The Samson Story

The Samson Story

Love, Seduction, Betrayal, Violence, Riddles, Myth

Shaul Bar

WIPF & STOCK · Eugene, Oregon

THE SAMSON STORY
Love, Seduction, Betrayal, Violence, Riddles, Myth

Copyright © 2018 Shaul Bar. All rights reserved. Except for brief quotations in critical publications or reviews, no part of this book may be reproduced in any manner without prior written permission from the publisher. Write: Permissions, Wipf and Stock Publishers, 199 W. 8th Ave., Suite 3, Eugene, OR 97401.

Wipf & Stock
An Imprint of Wipf and Stock Publishers
199 W. 8th Ave., Suite 3
Eugene, OR 97401

www.wipfandstock.com

PAPERBACK ISBN: 978-1-5326-4649-2
HARDCOVER ISBN: 978-1-5326-4650-8
EBOOK ISBN: 978-1-5326-4651-5

Manufactured in the U.S.A.

This book is dedicated to my dear uncle, Sidney Shlomo Wilgowicz,
Z"L.
A generous, kind, very special person whom I miss dearly.

Contents

Acknowledgements | ix
Abbreviations | x
Introduction | xv

1. The Birth of Samson | 1
   Samson's Parents | 2
   Manoah's Wife and the Messenger | 5
   Manoah's Wife Report | 6
   The Angel's Second Appearance | 9
   The Purpose of the Story | 15

2. Nazirite | 19
   Law of the Nazirite | 20
   Samson in Light of the Biblical Law | 24
   Samuel in Light of the Biblical Law | 26
   Samson's Mother | 28
   Hannah, Samuel's mother | 28
   Nazir in the Bible | 30
   Origin of Nazirite Law | 32

3. Literary Structure | 35
   The Birth of Samson | 36
   A Broken Vow | 40
   Chapters 14–15 | 42
   The Downfall | 46
   Samson and the Book of Samuel | 49

Contents

4. Women in the Samson Story | 52
    The Timnite Woman | 53
    Pressuring Samson's Wife | 58
    The Harlot from Gaza | 62
    Samson and Delilah | 64

5. Samson's Riddle | 71
    Riddles in the Hebrew Bible | 71
    Samson's Riddle | 74
    The Philistines' Riddle | 79
    Samson's Reply | 81

6. Mythical Elements in the Samson Story | 84
    Samson Kills a Lion | 85
    Jawbone of an Ass | 88
    The Gates of Gaza | 89
    Samson and the Foxes | 90
    Solar Myth | 92
    Sun Worship | 95

7. Philistines | 97
    The People and their Origin | 97
    Philistines and the Tribe of Dan | 99
    The First Clashes with the Philistines | 100
    The Philistines During the Reign of David and Salomon | 101
    The Culture of the Philistines | 103

8. The Death of Samson | 112
    The Philistines' Jubilation | 113
    Samson's Revenge | 117
    The Burial of Samson | 120

Conclusion | 123

Bibliography | 129
Index | 135

Acknowledgment

To start with, I would like to thank my two readers who read the early drafts of the manuscript and offered many perceptive and insightful comments: Anna S. Chernak, who read the initial manuscript and offered valuable advice with continuous encouragement, then Bob Turner, Circulation Librarian at the Harding School of Theology, who made many suggestions and offered his wisdom. I am grateful as well to Shoshana Cenker who read the final draft of the manuscript.

I want to express appreciation to the staff of the Harding School of Theology in Memphis. Librarian Don Meredith led me to many resources, Associate Librarian Sheila Owen helped me with research, and Evelyn Meredith supported my efforts with inspiration.

Special thanks to Hebrew Union College Library in New York City, where Head Librarian Yoram Bitton provided me with all the necessary help, wisdom, as well as friendship, and Librarian Tina Weiss who helped with my research.

Finally, a special thanks to the people at Wipf & Stock for their devotion and expertise in transforming my manuscript into this book.

Shaul Bar
Memphis, Tennessee
February 2018

Abbreviations

AB	Anchor Bible
ABD	*The Anchor Bible Dictionary*. 6 vols. Edited by D.N. Freedman New York: Doubleday, 1992.
AJBA	*Australian Journal of Biblical Archaeology*
ANET	*Ancient Near Eastern Texts Relating to the Old Testament*. 3rd ed. Edited by J.B. Pritchard. Princeton: Princeton University Press, 1969.
Ant	Josephus, Flavius. *Jewish Antiquities*. Translated by H. St. J. Thackeray. Cambridge, MA: Harvard University Press, 1930.
AOSup	Aula orientalis Supplementa
ATD	Das Alte Testament Deutsch.
b.	Babylonian Talmud
B. Bat.	*Baba Batra*
B. Meṣ	*Baba Meṣi'a*
BA	*Biblical Archaeologist*
Ber	*Berakhot*
BethM	*Beth Miqra:* Journal for the study of the Bible and Its World
BHS³	*Biblia hebraica stuttgartensia,* ed. K. Elliger and W. Rudolf, Stuttgart 1969-1975, 1984.
Bib	*Biblica*

Abbreviations

CBQ	*Catholic Biblical Quarterly*
DDD	*Dictionary of Deities and Demons in the Bible.* Ed. K. van der Toorn, B. Becking, and P.W. van der Horst, Leiden, 1995.
EncJud	*Encyclopedia Judaica.* 2ec ed. 22 vols. Edited by Fred Skolnik. Jerusalem: Keter, 2007.
Gen. R.	*Genesis Rabbah*
HSM	Harvard Semitic Monographs
ICC	International Critical Commentary
IDB	*The Interpreter's Dictionary of the Bible.* 4vols. Edited by George ArthurButtrick. Nashville: Abingdon, 1962.
Il	Homer. *The Illiad*
J. Ta'an	Jerusalem Ta'anit
JBL	*Journal of Biblical Literature*
JCS	*Journal of Cuneiform Studies*
JETS	*Journal of the Evangelical Theological Society*
JHS	*Journal of Hebrew Scripture*
TJ	Jerusalem Talmud
JNSL	*Journal of Northwest Semitic Languages*
JQR	*Jewish Quarterly Review*
JRAS	*Journal of the Royal Asiatic Society*
JSOT	*Journal for the Study of the Old Testament*
JSOTSup	Journal for the study of the Old Testament Supplement Series
JTS	*Journal of Theological Studies*
Ketub	*Ketubbot*
Lev. R.	Leviticus Rabbah
LXX	Septuagint
M. Tem	*Mishnah Temurah*

Abbreviations

1Mac	1Maccabees
Mish	Mishnah
Naz	*Nazir*
Ned	*Nedarim*
NIB	*The New Interpreter's Bible*
Nid	*Niddah*
NJB	New Jerusalem Bible
Num. R.	*Numbers Rabbah*
Od.	Homer. *The Odyssey*
OTE	Old Testament Essays
PEQ	Palestine Exploration Quarterly
Proof	*Prooftexts: A Journal of Jewish Literary History*
Roš Haš	*Roš Haššanah*
Shnaton	*Shnaton: An annual for Biblical and ancient Near Eastern Studies*
Soṭah	*Soṭah*
Tarbiz	*Tarbiz*
TDOT	*Theological Dictionary of the Old Testament.* 14. vols. Edited by G. Johannes Botterweck and Helmer Ringgren. Translated by Geoffrey W. Bromiley et al. Grand Rapids: Eerdmans, 1974-2004.
Tosef.	Tosefta
UJE	*The Universal Jewish Encyclopedia,* 10 vols. Edited by Isaac Landman. New York: Universal Jewish Encyclopedia, 1939-43.
VE	*Vox evangelica*
VT	*Vetus Testamentum*
VTSup	VT Supplement Series
Vulg	Vulgate

Abbreviations

WBC	Word Biblical Commentary
y.	Jerusalem Talmud
Yisrael	*Ozar Yisrael An Encyclopedia*. 10 Volumes. Edited by J.D. Eisenstein. New York: J.D. Eisenstein, 1913.
ZAW	*Zeitschrift für alttestamentliche Wissenschaft*
ZDMG	*Zeitschrift der deutschen morgenländischen Gesellschaft*

Introduction

THE BOOK OF JUDGES received its name because many judges are the main characters in this book. These narratives describe to us the period between the death of Joshua and the arrival of Samuel, which is a period of transition and crisis. The Israelites failed to deal effectively with the Canaanites; they are still in the process of conquering the promised land. Men are reluctant to assume leadership roles; the tribes act independently and are not coming to aid each other in times of crisis and war (Judg. 5:17; 21:9). In addition, they are also fighting against each other (21:20). There are repeated statements about the lack of justice and righteousness. "Everyone did what was right in his own eyes" prevailed among the Israelites because there was no king. The author describes murder, war, strife among brothers, rape, and cultic sins. In light of the calamity that is described in the Book of Judges it was suggested: "The purpose of the work was to show that a centralized hereditary kingship was necessary for the well-being of the Covenant theocracy."[1]

The author of the book remains anonymous. Talmudic tradition identified the author as Samuel: "Samuel wrote the book which bears his name and the Book of Judges, and Ruth."[2] But examination of the book reveals that there are signs of gradual growth in the narrative from isolated stories to late additions. Since the stories about the judges are not equal in length, scholars use different terms for the judges. Heroes that the book describes in length are called "major" Judges, this includes: Othniel, Ehud, Deborah, Gideon, Jephthah, and Samson. On the other hand, those who are barely described are called "minor": Shamgar, Tola, Jair, Ibzan, Elon, and Abdon. No acts of deliverance are attributed to them; there is only a reference to

---

1. Harrison, *Introduction to the Old Testament*, 692.
2. *b. B. Bat. 14b*.

Introduction

their family and that they judged Israel, and where their graves were to be found. Although the heroes of the book are designated as judges, none of them were judges in the legal sense. Their main function was a military role and sometimes they acted as civil rulers. The only exception is Deborah, whom the Israelites came to for judgment (Judg 4:4). Another term that described the role of the leaders in the Book of Judges is מושיע *môšîa* "deliverer/liberator," which is applied to Othniel, Ehud, Shamagar, Gideon, Tola, Jephthah, and Samson. Their mission was to deliver the Israelites from the hand of their enemy. Hence, we read about Samson: "He shall be the first to deliver Israel from the Philistines" (Judg 13:5).

Scholars maintain that the core of Judges 2:6–16:31 was the final work of the Deuteronomic editors. These editors created a theme that united the stories with a recurring pattern. Israel sinned by following other gods; as a result God subjected them to a foreign oppressor. The Israelites repented and prayed for God to deliver them. God sent a judge to liberate them from their oppressor. The judge achieved his mission, which is followed by a peaceful period. After the death of the judge, people again followed other gods and the cycle repeats itself. Hence, in the Samson story: "The Israelites again did what was offensive to the Lord, and the Lord delivered them into the hands of the Philistines for forty years" (Judg13:1).

Samson is the last of the judges. Twenty percent of the Book of Judges is devoted to Samson, which is more space for him than any of the other judges. The story of Samson is a true reflection of his times: "In those days there was no king in Israel; every man did as he pleased" (Judg 17:6; 21:25). Each tribe was fighting against their individual enemies. The Philistines oppressed the Israelites for a long time and their suzerainty was also recognized by Israel (14:4; 15:11). This is in contrast to previous stories where the Israelites cried under the burden of oppression; here the coexistence with the Philistines became the norm. The Philistines are destined to become the most serious enemy of the Israelites. Samson's fighting with the Philistines foreshadows the fights that Saul would have with the Philistines in the future. Samson is the hero of his tribe and, as such, he is supposed to deliver his people. The only Israelite enemy who is mentioned twice in the Book of Judges is the Philistines. They are first mentioned when they are defeated by Shamgar who killed 600 Philistines with an ox goad (Judg 3:31), and they are mentioned again when Samson fights against them time after time.

Samson is a unique judge, as he does not lead his people into battle he acts alone; his battles are a personal vendetta. Unlike other judges, Samson

Introduction

has a weakness for women, in particular, foreign Philistine women. This has led scholars to believe that the author wanted to present the reader with a person with a weak make up.[3] But this is not the case with Samson who is different from the typical Israelite judges. Buber noted that "it is the weak and the humble who are chosen" for leadership.[4] Hence, Deborah is a woman, and Gideon is the youngest son of the weakest clan in the tribe of Manasseh (Judg 6:15). Jephthah is a son of a prostitute. On the other hand, Samson is a consecrated Nazirite with enormous strength who does not have all these limitations. Nevertheless, unlike Jephthah who keeps a vow, Samson breaks his. While the other stories in the Book of Judges end with triumph, the end of the Samson story is tragic. Samson lost his strength and only regained it in order to die. Despite his heroic victories, he did not remove the Philistines' oppression. His single-handed battles were successful, but only many years later the threat from the Philistines was removed.

No other judge received such elaborate attention as Samson. However, he is not mentioned again in the Hebrew Bible. This is puzzling since some of the judges and some of the historical events that took place are mentioned later in the biblical narrative. Hence, the Book of Psalms mentioned the great deliverance from Sisera and Jabin, Oreb and Zeev, Zebah and Zalmunna (Ps 83:10–12). The Prophet Isaiah mentioned the victory against Midian (9:3; 10:26). More so, when the prophet Samuel summarized the history of Israel in his last speech (chap. 12), he cited some of its previous enemies and the names of the judges who delivered Israel. Samson is absent from the list; instead we read of an unknown personality by the name of Dan. Hence, Targum Jonathan identified Dan with Samson. Likewise, we read in the Talmud: "And why is he called Bedan? Because he comes from the tribe of Dan" in other words, Bedan is a contraction of "a son of Dan," which refers to Samson.[5] Another allusion to Samson might be found in Jacob's blessing. Jacob on the eve of his death blessed his sons, among them the tribe of Dan (Gen 49:16-18). The sages' interpreted verse 18 as alluding to Samson: "wait for Your deliverance, O Lord!"

In contrast to the Old Testament, Samson is mentioned in the New Testament in Hebrew 11:32: "And what shall I more say? For the time would fail me to tell of Gideon, and of Barak, and of Samson, and of Jephthah; of David also, and Samuel, and of the prophets." In other words, the New

---

3. Crenshaw, *Samson*, 141-43; Kraft, "Samson," In *IDB* 4:20.
4. Buber, *On the Bible*, 141–42.
5. b. Roš Haš.25a.

Introduction

Testament places Samson with other favorable judges and the great personage of antiquity, not passing any negative judgment on him. We should stress that although some of these men are not portrayed in favorable ways in the Old Testament, nevertheless, they showed their faith in God and were able to deliver their people from external enemies. The fact that Samson did not deliver Israel from the Philistines and is not mentioned in the later books of the Bible led to the thinking that he did not deserve to be included among the judges. Therefore, it is suggested that his inclusion in the Book of Judges is to ensure that there were 12 judges. More so, the writing style and his biography appear to have originated from a different source, which is again different from the previous chapters of the Book of Judges.[6]

Noth offered another explanation for why Samson is not mentioned later in the Hebrew Bible. He also pointed to the fact that Samson's name is missing from 1Samuel 12 "a passage which clearly aims to be comprehensive."[7] According to him, the Deuteronomist usually mentioned only one savior during the oppression of foreign rule. Hence, it was Samuel and not Samson who fulfilled this savior role in light of the Philistines' oppression, which is mentioned in Judges 13:1. Noth said that it is difficult to decide if the Dtr's account included the Samson stories or maybe they are interpolated later. Although Noth did not dismiss the possibility that Samson's story was part of the Dueteronomistic history, nevertheless, he considered it unlikely.[8]

A positive evaluation of Samson appears in Josephus' writings. According to him, Samson was a man of astonishing qualities, the exception being his relationships with women. He said: "That he let himself be ensnared by a woman must be imputed to human nature which succumbs to sins; but testimony is due to him for his surpassing excellence in all the rest."[9] Josephus was most impressed by Samson's courage for dying. But this is not surprising since he himself broke an agreement to commit suicide.

In Rabbinic literature, Samson is identified with Bedan, in other words, he was called this because he was from the tribe of Dan.[10] His name is derived from שמש *shemesh* (sun), so Samson has the same name as God who is also "a sun and shield,"(Ps.84:12); as God protected Israel so did

---

6. Cohen, "Samson," In *UJE* 9:341.
7. Noth, *Deuteronomistic History*, 52
8. Ibid.
9. Josephus, *Ant.* 5. 317.
10. *Roš Haš.* 25A

Introduction

Samson. The strength of Samson is from God, therefore, as God, he does not require any assistance so Samson fought his battles alone.[11] The width between Samson's shoulders was 60 cubits. He was lame in both feet, but when the spirit of God seized him, he could step with one stride from Zorah to Esthol.[12] Also when the Holy Spirit rested on him, he released a bell-like sound that could be heard from afar. He was so strong that he could uproot two mountains and grind one against the other.[13] In his lust for women, he is compared to Amnon and Zimri who were both punished for their sins.[14] During the years that he judges Israel, he never mentioned the name of God in vain. Therefore, when he told Delilah that he was a Nazarite of God, she immediately recognized that he spoke the truth. When he died at the temple of Dagon, killing himself and many Philistines, the structure fell backward. In other words, he was not crushed so his family could find his body and bury him in his father's tomb. It appears that all those details of Samson's heroic deeds led the sages of the Talmudic era to deny the belief that Samson was a historic figure. In other words, they thought that he was purely a mythological figure. Nevertheless, this heresy eventually was rejected in the Talmud.[15]

Several monographs have been written on the whole or part of the Samson cycle. Among the recent manuscripts we find: James L. Crenshaw's, *Samson: A Secret Betrayed, a Vow Ignored* (1978), which analyzes the story through a literary prism. Yair Zakovitch's, *The Samson Story* (1982), examines the story through a close reading of the Biblical text, analyzing each verse separately; Jichan Kim's, *The Structure of the Samson Cycle* (1993), studies the structure and narrative development; and Pnina Galpaz-Feller's, *The Women Be Upon Thee, Samson* (2003), uses associative analysis by comparing this story with other cultural stories from the Ancient Near East.

In addition, through the years, important commentaries and monographs were written on the Book of Judges among them: C.F. Burney's, *The Book of Judges* (1920); Robert G. Boling's, *Judges* (1969); J. Alberto Soggin's, *Judges* (1981); Trent C. Butler's, *Judges*, (2009); Barry G. Webb's, *The Book of Judges* (2012); Yairah Amit's, *The Book of Judges: The Art of Editing* (1999); and Marc Zvi Brettler's, *The Book of Judges* (2002).

11. Gen. R.98:13
12. b. Soṭah. 10a
13. b. Soṭah. 9b.
14. Lev. R. 23:9.
15. b. B. Bat. 91a; Eisenstein, "Samson," In *Yisrael* 10:191.

Introduction

In this book, my main goal is to rediscover Samson, to have a better understanding of his personality, his achievements, and failures. Hence, I will describe Samson from these different facets. In order to achieve this goal, we will use the synchronic method, analyzing the texts as it stands, comparing its language motifs and ideas to the other Biblical texts. This, in turn, will shed more light on the persona of Samson. Additionally, in order to have a better understanding into the Samson cycle, material found in the Talmud, the Midrashim, and the Jewish medieval commentators will be reviewed. The Talmud contains a vast amount of *aggadot*—stories. The Midrash includes anthologies and compilations of homilies including Biblical exegesis and public sermons. The various sects and currents in Judaism left their mark on these and almost everything that Jews thought during a period of more than 1,000 years can be found there. Though the interpretative methods of the medieval commentators vary, we still find that they compromise between the literal and the Midrashic interpretations of the Biblical text. In addition, they pursue philological-contextual interpretations with a reasoned and science perspective.

The story of the birth of Samson has some similarities to other Biblical stories, which deal with the motif of "barrenness," such as: Sarah, Rebecca, and Rachel. This motif is also found in the New Testament, which certainly was influenced by the Hebrew Bible with stories about the birth of John the Baptist and Jesus. These types of stories were also prevalent in the mythical world with stories about the birth of Hercules and Orion. Examination of myth from the ancient world shows that they contained legends dealing with divine people. Samson's mother is the only one who received two visits from an angel who informed her on the birth of her son. While Abraham asked for a son, no such request came from Manoah or his wife. Also missing from our story is the element of the mockery of barren women by a rival wife or handmaid, which occurred in the Sarah, Rachel, and Hannah stories. Samson is the only judge of whom the narrator described his birth in such detail. Hence, the inevitable question that needs to be asked in chapter 1 is: Why did the narrator attach such importance to the description of Samson's birth? Furthermore, by describing Samson's birth, what did the author try to achieve?

In chapter 2 we investigate the Nazirite concept. While receiving the news about the future birth of her son, the angel told Samson's mother that her son would be a Nazirite. This is the only place in the Hebrew Bible where a Nazirite vow is imposed by someone outside of the family. Under

Introduction

different circumstances it is done voluntarily (Num 6:1-21), or it is a vow that was taken by the mother (1Sam 1:11). Being a Nazirite meant that the person was close to Yahweh. It entails restrictions such as: abstaining from any product from the vine; to allow the hair on his head to grow untrimmed; and to avoid contact with a corpse. Hence, in this chapter we will examine the theme of the Nazirite vow. We will analyze the characters of Samson, Samuel, Samson's mother, and Hannah to see if, indeed, they follow those restrictions and were Nazirite. In addition, we will study the subject of the Nazirites in the Hebrew Bible to try to understand the reasoning and origin for this custom.

In chapter 3 we study the literary structure of the Samson story. Examination of the story reveals that there are three major blocks: 1) The birth account (13:1–25); 2) the parallel life accounts (14:1–15:20); and 3) the death account (16:1–31). The story starts with the birth of Samson and ends with his death. In addition, the geographic boundaries are set, Samson operates between Zorah and Eshtaol. The spirit of the Lord seized him there, and he was buried there. In spite of the structural frame of the story, scholars maintain that the various tales about Samson were initially retold separately and only afterward collected and arranged to create a story about the hero Samson. According to Fohrer, the Samson stories include self-sufficient narratives and anecdotes that were loosely linked together, these stories were incorporated into the Book of Judges in two stages.[16] Kratz maintained that the core tradition is found in Judges 14:1–15.8. In this tradition various stages were added, which include the etiology of the place Ramath-lehi in Judah in 15:9–19, the continuation of the story about the women, the harlot, and Delilah in 16:1–30, and the birth legend in 13:2–24. To integrate the independent narrative into the Book of Judges, Deuteronomistic elements incorporated in 13:1, 5, 25; 14:6, 19; 15:4, 20; 16:31 where "the shadow of Saul may be recognized in Samson."[17] Römer claimed that the Book of Judges has the least typical Deuteronomistic passages, although it was slightly reworked by the Deuteronomistic school. The stories about

---

16. The first group of stories includes 13;2–25, Samson's birth; chapter 14 Samson's marriage and the riddle; 15:1–8 Samson burns the grain of the Philistines; 15:9–19 Samson kills the Philistines with the jawbone of an ass. At the end of this group, we find a concluding formula in 15:20; this is followed by a second group that was added later in 16:1–3, Samson at Gaza; 16:4–22, Samson and Delilah; 16:23–31a, Samson's death, 16:31b, which is the second concluding formula. See: Fohrer, *Introduction to the Old Testament*, 211.

17. Kratz, *Composition of the Narrative Books*, 205.

Introduction

the judges, except Othniel, came from the Northern kingdom. The Samson stories reveal Hellenistic influences as well as the Judges 17–18 and 19–21. These stories are post-Deuteronomistic pieces that were added in order to create an independent Book of Judges without the Samuel stories. According to him, it is not clear if the Samson stories were integrated before, later, or at the same time as chapters 17–21, which had a negative conclusion to the Book of Judges with stories about sex and crimes.[18] Olson also maintains that the Samson stories were added later to the Book of Judges. He pointed out the extensive number of motifs that the writers or editors have borrowed from the earlier stories in the Book of Judges. He mentions 16 insinuations from the Book of Judges that were incorporated in the Samson stories. Thus, he arrived at the conclusion that the Samson story was shaped and edited at a late stage of the book's completion, when most of the material in Judges was already written.[19] Hence, in the current chapter we examine these three blocks to see if they are in fact independent of each other or if there is a connection between those blocks that links them into one cohesive story.

One of the themes that repeats itself in the Hebrew Bible is the attraction to foreign women. Time after time Samson follows a Philistine woman who betrayed him. His weakness for women led him to reveal his secret and, ultimately, to his downfall. In the Hebrew Bible, a mighty hero who falls before a deceitful woman appears in several biblical narratives. Hence, we read of Jael, wife of Heber the Kenite, who offers hospitality to Sisera and then murders him (Judg 4:21). Haman is invited by Esther to her banquet and later he is hung from the tree that he prepared for Mordecai (Esth 7:10). Judith went to the camp of Holofernes, who was Nebuchadnezzar's commander in chief. He was attracted by her wisdom and beauty and invited her to a feast. When he fell asleep from heavy drinking, Judith took a knife and cut off his head. In the three stories, the women used their feminine charm, which led the hero to let his guard down. In these stories, it is a Jewish woman who saves her people from a foreigner, therefore, the sympathy of the reader is with her. Not so in the Samson story where he falls into a trap and reveals his secret to the foreign woman; here the sympathy is with Samson. It was suggested that the story was originally a Philistine story that came to glorify Delilah while mocking Samson.[20] Later

---

18. Römer, *The So-Called Deuteronomistic History*, 90–1, 136–39, 182.
19. Olson, "Judges," In *NIB* 2: 842.
20. Zakovit, *Life of Samson*, 194.

Introduction

the story was transformed into a Hebrew story, whereas the woman's act is not motivated by patriotism but by greed. The hero's defeat is not final, he received another chance to avenge his enemies with the aid of the God of Israel. Hence, in chapter four we examine Samson's involvement with the three foreign women and point out the different aspects of his involvement with them; in addition we will study their place and function in the Samson narrative.

Judges 14 gives us a graphic description of the wedding festivities in ancient Israel. Upon his marriage to the Timnite woman, Samson made a feast as was the custom. He told the Philistine men a riddle that involved a lion and honey. A wager was made on the riddle. This was not unusual since in the ancient world riddles were a source of entertainment, especially at banquets and celebrations in a king's court; it was a test of wisdom. In chapter 5, we will study the subjects of riddles in the Hebrew Bible. We will examine Samson's riddle to see if it has any links to the story of the lion and Samson eating the honey from its carcass. Alternatively, the riddle predates its present context, and Samson adapts the riddle to his private experience. Thus, we will analyze the different proposals for the origin of Samson's riddle. In addition, we will study the Philistines response to Samson's riddle. The Philistines gave their answer in the form of a question. The Philistines answer may itself disguise an earlier riddle about love. Finally, Samson's response to the Philistines includes erotic imagery that was well-known in the Ancient near East. Was there any reason for Samson to use this kind of language?

In chapter 6, we study the mythological elements of the Samson story. Some of the features in the Samson story contain some mythological elements. This led scholars to define the whole narrative as a "solar myth." Thus, his name is connected with *shemesh* "sun," his hair the "solar rays," and then he is blinded: "the sun is darkened." His birthplace was across the Valley of Sorek, a short distance from the city of Beth-Shemesh "house of sun," the site of a shrine of the sun god. There is also a resemblance to stories of heroes of the past such as Hercules and Orion from the Greeks and Gilgamesh from Mesopotamia. Like these mythical heroes, Samson fights with a lion, is defeated by women and is associated with two pillars. Hence, we study the alleged mythological elements that are found in our story. We compare Samson to mythological heroes of the ancient world to see if, indeed, Samson was a mythical hero.

Introduction

In chapter 7, we'll direct our attention to the Philistines who were the main foes of Samson. We survey their history as it is presented in the biblical narrative. We examine their origin and their places of habitat. Was there any connection between the Philistines and the tribe of Dan? In Genesis in the Testament of Jacob ,where he addresses his sons before his death, Jacob refers to Dan "like one of the tribes of Israel" (49:16). Therefore, it is possible that originally the tribe did not belong to the tribal confederation of Israel and joined them at a later time. The clashes between Samson and the Philistines were only the beginning of a long battle between the two people. These battles lasted for a long period until David finally defeated the Philistines. This crushing blow by David signals the end of the Philistine Pentapolis. To have a better read of the Philistines, we'll study their material culture and political organization. The formation of Pentapolis, which included five cities, was for political, commercial, and military reasons. So how were the cities ruled and organized? Who led the army and what kind of armament did the Philistines use. What was their livelihood: Were the Philistines farmers, shepherds, or merchants? Samson and the Philistines communicate freely, therefore, in what language did they speak? The Bible mentions several Philistine gods, so were they Semitic gods or gods the Philistines brought with them? What does archeology tells us about their temples and religious artifacts?

In the last chapter, we describe the last part of Samson's life including his death. It appears in such specific detail, which is not found with other judges. The first scene opens with the Philistines jubilation to Samson's fall, this includes two short poems one by the *seranim* and the second one by the people. So how different are these poems and what message do they convey? These poems are followed by Samson's prayer to God, which we will compare to his first prayer to God at Ramath-lehi and see how different the prayers are. In his prayer, Samson expressed a death wish, therefore, we will compare it to other death wishes and their outcome. The narrator ends the story by mentioning that his brothers and all his father's house came to pick up his body and that they buried him. Is there any significance for mentioning this and his burial site?

We trust that this study will provide a provocative and useful insight into the life of Samson.

1

The Birth of Samson

THIS STORY STARTS WITH the birth announcement of Samson, which is a glaring contrast to other stories in the Book of Judges, where the judges first appear as adults. Accordingly, the angel appeared to Samson's mother and informed her that she would conceive a son and he would be the first one to deliver Israel from the hands of the Philistines. In other words, Samson is destined, even before his birth, to deliver Israel. Examination of the stories in the Book of Judges reveals that these stories follow a pattern; the Israelites are oppressed, they cry to the Lord, and He sends a judge to deliver them. Customarily, the narrator gives the reader a reason for the elections of the Judge. Therefore, Othniel the Kenizzite was a younger kinsman of Caleb (Judg 3:9); Ehud son of Gera appears as a brave man; Deborah the Prophetess chooses Barak by a command from God (4:6); Gideon worried about the people of Israel (6:12); Jephthah the Gileadite was an able warrior (11:1). In this story, Samson is chosen to deliver Israel without any apparent explanation. In all previous episodes, the appeal to Yahweh is mentioned, but it is missing from the Samson story. Hence, why is this story so vastly different from other stories in the Book of Judges? Webb suggested that the story came to demonstrate that the power of God, barrenness and fertility, and life and death are all in the hands of Yahweh.[1] While this is the case in many other biblical stories, it does not explain the uniqueness of the birth of Samson.[2] Some other scholars suggested that the story came to compare Manoah to his wife, as well as portraying him as inferior to his wife.[3] This

---

1. Webb, *Judges*, 167.
2. Assis, "Significance of the Narrative," 22.
3. Exum, "Promise and Fulfillment," 43–59; Niditch, "Samson as Culture Hero," 610–12.

might be true in some parts of the story. Still, the bigger question left unanswered is the placement of Samson's birth story in the biblical narrative. In other words, is there any connection between the birth narrative and the rest of Samson's story? What kind of message is the narrator trying to convey by recounting the birth of Samson and for what purpose? We believe that answering these questions will help us understand the reason for the inclusion of the birth narrative in the Samson cycle. More so, this will help us understand the placement of the Samson story in the Book of Judges.

Samson's Parents

The story of the birth of Samson is one of the ancient stories in the Hebrew Bible. The story is similar to Genesis 18 and to Judges 6:11–24. These stories describe the appearance of God or his angels during the day disguised as humans. In addition, a meal is mentioned. In Genesis, the meal is eaten, whereas in Judges 6 it is only served. And, in our story, it is only offered. In Judges 6, the purpose of the theophany is to send Gideon on a mission to save his people. Not so in Genesis 18 and the Samson story, where the theophany serves as an announcement to a barren woman that she would conceive a son. There is bewilderment, so questions are raised about the validity of the messages that were given. Hence, Sarah is laughing after hearing that she will become pregnant. Gideon is asking for proof or a sign and so does Manoah.

Like other stories in the Book of Judges, the story of Samson's birth starts with an editorial note: "The Israelites again did what was offensive to the Lord, and the Lord delivered them into the hands of the Philistines for forty years" (Judg 13:1). The Israelites were to be blamed for their situation. The formula "did what was offensive to the Lord," opens the description of the Judges period (2:11) and appears here for the last time. This is a Deuteronomistic formula that is mentioned in the Book of Deuteronomy (9:18; 17:2 31: 29), and in the Book of Judges, and over 40 times in the Book of Kings. The nature of the Israelite offence is not revealed. The Israelites were oppressed by the Philistines for 40 years. Evidently, this continued after Samson's death. For the first time the Israelites were not liberated during the life span of their judge. The period of 40 years is repeated in the Book of Judges. Three times: "the land had peace for 40 years" (Judg 3:11; 5:31; 8:28). The number is a round number mentioned many times in the Hebrew Bible, therefore, it does not contribute to the chronological validity of the story.[4] In previous stories, we find a cry for help (3; 9, 15; 4:3; 6:6; 10:15), but this element is missing from our story. Thus, it was suggested that the Israelites did not cry for help since they accepted the Philistines as their overlords.[5]

Following the editorial note, the narrator introduces Manoah and his wife. This kind of introduction is similar to other biblical stories such as the Samuel story (1Sam 1:1–2) and Saul's story (9:1). What is interesting here is that the hero is not mentioned, only his parents. Manoah is from Zorah, a town situated 18 miles west of Jerusalem in the low hill country where the Philistines had settled.[6] The town will be mentioned again after the birth of Samson (Judg. 13:25) and in the final chapter of his life (16:31). Manoah is from a family משפחת (*mišpaḥat*) of the Danites. The narrator's description did not use the word tribe. This is probably because not all of Dan's tribesman lived in the vicinity of Zorah. Another explanation might be that the tribe consisted of one family (Num 26:42). It is also noteworthy that the terms for family and tribe are used interchangeably (18:19). Possibly by using the word family, it was a way for the narrator to point out that Manoah came from a weak marginal group. The Samson cycle is set in the southern part of the land of Israel prior to the migration of the tribe to the north.[7] Manoah is identified by town and tribe. He is the only male in the Books of Judges and 1Samuel who is not mentioned with paternal connection as Ehud (Judg. 3:15), Barak (4:6), Gideon (6:11), Abimelech (9:1), Jotham (9:5), Gaal (9:26), Jephthah (11:1), Samuel's father Elkanah (1Sam1:1), and Saul's father Kish (9:1).[8]

The name Manoah means "rest." The name of his wife, on the other hand, is not mentioned at all and she remained nameless. This is similar to other stories in the Book of Judges such as Micah's mother, the daughter of Jephthah, and the concubine in Gibeah. Reinhartz pointed out that the

---

4. For forty year the Israelites wandered in the desert (Num 14:33–4; 32:13); Eli Judged Israel for forty years (1Sam 4:18); David ruled Israel for forty years (1Kgs 2:11); the flood lasted for forty days (Gen 7:17); Moses stayed forty days on Mount Sinai (Exod 24:18; 34:28; Deut 10:10). See: Moore, *Judges*, xxxvii–xliii.

5. Crenshaw, *Samson*, 40.

6. In Joshua it is listed as a town of Judah (15:33), while in 19:41 as a city that belonged to the tribe of Dan. However, later the Danites migrated north and the city became a town of Judah.

7. The story of Deborah in Judges 4–5 on the other hand assumes that the tribe had already moved to the north. See: Kaufman, *Judges*, 56.

8. Greenstein, "Riddle of Samson," 240–41.

angel also remains nameless in the story. This fact led her to believe that there is a link between the two. According to her, the fact that Samson's mother remains unnamed points to her central role in the story.[9] The sages, on the other hand, gave her the name *Hatzlallponie,* and she is from the tribe of Judah (1Chr 4:3).[10] We should point out that in the other biblical stories of barren women like Sarah, Rebecca, Rachel, and Samuel's mother Hannah, the names of these barren women are mentioned. Thus, it is possible that by avoiding a name for Samson's mother, it was a way to belittle the significance of the family.

It is interesting that in this text neither his father nor mother prayed nor requested to have a child. Therefore, Josephus added some details about the notable origin of Manoah and a prayer that he uttered to God: "But having no children by her and being distressed at the lack of them, he was wont, on his frequent visit with his wife to the outskirt—where there was a great plain to—entreat God to give them offspring of their wedlock."[11] Asis, on the other hand, suggested that the lack of mentioning any prayer by Samson's parents was the narrator's way to stress that the pregnancy was a result of God's grace and not because of Samson's parent's righteousness.[12]

Another important detail is that there is no information on the woman's particular situation:

> We are not told that she was old, as Sarah was (Gen 18:12). Nor does she complain to her husband about childlessness, as does Rachel (30:1). We are not informed that she tries other means of procuring a child, as Sarah and Rachel do, when they give their maids to their husbands (16:3; 30:3). Nor does she turn to aphrodisiacs, as Rachel apparently does in Genesis 30:14–24. The text does not report that the woman prays for children, as does Hannah (1Sam 1:11), nor that her husband prays for her, as Isaac prays for Rebekah (Gen 25:21).[13]

Although Manoah's wife's name is missing from the text, she receives a message from a mysterious messenger of Yahweh. There is no explanation of why she merited such revelation. Hence, the sages pointed out that Manoah's wife was righteous because she merited an angel speaking to

---

9. Reinhartz, "Samson's Mother," 25–37.
10. *b. B. Bat. 91a*
11. Josephus, *Ant.* 5.276.
12. Assis, "Significance of the Narrative," 33
13. Exum, "Promise and Fulfillment," 47–8.

her.[14] More so, she was from the tribe of Judah, which instilled the child with leadership qualities and the potential to be a Nazirite. By contrast, her husband was from the lowly tribe of Dan.[15] Abravanel (Isaac ben Judah 1437–1508) suggests that she possessed more wisdom than her husband (v.23), therefore, the angel appeared to her. Given that the angel appeared to her with the restrictions to avoid strong drink and unclean food, these were given to her first and later to her husband.

Manoah's Wife and the Messenger

In his message to Manoah's wife, the messenger told her: "You will become pregnant and bear a son." This is in contrast to her current situation where: "Right now, you are barren and have no children." The announcement is similar to other biblical stories where the barren were informed about their future pregnancy: Sarah, Rebecca, Rachel, and Hannah (Gen 18:3; 25:22; 30:22; 1Sam 1:17). However, in our story, in addition to his declaration, the messenger also imposed restrictions on her. Accordingly, she would not drink any wine or any intoxicating beverage and also would not eat unclean food. All of this is because her future son would be a Nazirite for God from the womb. Furthermore, a baby nourishes from that which he eats from his mother, therefore, the restrictions were imposed on her too.[16]

The prohibition against drinking any wine or intoxicating beverage is typical to Nazirite law (Num 6:3). Hence, here the narrator mentions the drinking first in contrast to the biblical narrative that usually mentions eating before drinking (Deut 2:6; 29:5; 1Sam 30:12, 16). Abravanel pointed out that Samson's abstentions from wine would remove any notion that he was drunk when he behaved strangely. According to Ralbag (Rabbi Levi ben Gershom 1248–1344), since Samson went after his eyes, God made him a Nazirite because wine leads to lewdness. More so, God made him Nazirite from birth to help Samson curb his desires.

In a previous announcement, such as in the Hagar story, the angel told her that she would conceive and bear a son and his name would be Ishmael. The angel also explained the meaning of the name to her. Similarly, the prophet Isaiah told the king of Judah that he would have a son named Immanuel (Isa 7:14). Not so in this story, where the name of the child is

14. *Num. R 10.*
15. *Gen. R. 98.*
16. *b. Nid. 30b.*

not given by God, it is the mother who gave Samson his name without explaining it (v.24).

Following the prohibitions that were given directly to Manoah's wife, the angel also gave her specific instructions about her future son. A razor must never come upon his head for the boy is to be a Nazirite for God from the womb. The same language is repeated with Samuel (1Sam 1:11). In the Hebrew Bible, it is only Samuel who was given a lifelong Nazirite vow from God (1Sam 1:11, 21). Samson and Samuel are lifelong Nazirites, this is in contrast to the biblical law that limits the time of Nazirite status. However, in the Samuel story, it was his mother Hannah's initiative when she took a vow that her future son would be a lifelong Nazirite. Still, we should point out that there is no difference between the two and the restrictions are identical. Greene pointed to the use of a razor and according to him: ". . . there is some particular reason for mentioning razor." [17] It is the razor that would bring the downfall of Samson, thus foreshadowing his future. Yet Abravanel explains that his unshaved head was a sign of grief and mourning because Israel was subjected to the Philistines' rule. He further points out that Samson's Nazarite conduct was the opposite of the Philistines who ate unclean food and indulged in wine. Therefore, not surprisingly, he was constantly contending with them.

The narrator ended the first encounter between Manoah's wife and the messenger with the messenger's words: "He shall be the first to deliver Israel from the Philistines" (Judg 13:5). This is exegetical comment made by the Deuteronmistic editor of the book. He tells the reader what Samson's accomplishment will be. He will not completely deliver Israel; he will only start the movement and his successes will be limited. This is the beginning of the end of the Philistines' oppression of Israel, which grew with intensity and reached its climax during the time of King Saul. As a result, the Israelites turned to Samuel and asked him for a king who would fight against the Philistines. Interestingly, the narrator does not describe how Manoah's wife reacted upon receiving the news that she would have a son who would deliver Israel. She remains passive throughout, as she is only a listener.

Manoah's Wife Report

With the disappearance of the angel of God, Manoah's wife went to her husband and told him: "A man of God came to me" (v.6). The narrator

---

17. Greene, "Enigma Variations," 59.

already revealed to the reader that it was an angel of God. It is only later when the angel of God leaves Manoah and his wife that they realize it was indeed an angel of God who appeared to them. The man of God appeared in the image of man. This is similar to other instances such as the appearances to Abraham and Lot (Gen 18–19) and to Gideon (Judg 6:11–24). The woman described his appearance like the appearance of an angel of God. Evidently, she did not comprehend that it was an inhuman who appeared to her. Nevertheless, his appearance left his mark on her as "totally awesome." That is why she was afraid to ask him where he was from and for his name. According to Ehrlich, "Because he looked like an angel of God . . . since she was sure that he was from heaven."[18] This is in contrast to Gideon who asked for a sign of truthfulness. It is only Manoah, her husband, who will later ask him for his name (v.17) in order to pay him back should his message be fulfilled. A question about the identity of the person and his place of origin was common (2Sam 1:13).

In addition to the description of the man of God, the woman also repeated his message to her husband. Repetition is a well-known tool of ancient world literature; it is found already in Akkadian, Ugaritic, and Greek literature. We have to remember that the ancient people gathered to hear stories and they enjoyed hearing plots that they were familiar with.[19] Still, there are several additions and omissions to her report. As Chisholm points out, Samson's mother failed to reveal to her husband the divinely appointed destiny of her son.[20] She did not mention that he would save Israel from the fear that the Philistines would hear about it and kill the child. More so, she did not mention the command to protect herself, as well as the prohibition of a razor ever passing over her son's head. The omission of a razor might be because she remarked that he would be a Nazirite. On the other hand, she added a phrase that was not mentioned before: "until the day of his death" (13:7). This was not mentioned by the messenger for the simple reason that he knew that Samson would break his Nazirite status before his death. Indeed, in the end, it would be the violation of the Nazirite law that led to Samson's downfall and death. As Abravanel pointed out, Manoah's wife did not want to put her husband to shame by telling him all the details of the child and his destiny because this would imply that she was greater than Manoah. Therefore, she mentioned only those details pertaining to

---

18. Ehrlich, *Mikrâ Ki-Pheschutô*, 2:77.
19. Cassuto, *Goddess Anath*, 34.
20. Chisholm, "What's Wrong with This Picture?," 177.

her conduct during her pregnancy, explaining that the child was to be a lifelong Nazirite. When Manoah's wife describes the messages she received about the child to her husband, he did not reply. His lack of comments might suggest that he looked down on her.[21]

The announcement of the birth of Samson is similar to a 'call' narrative in which a person is called to deliver his people. In this respect, our story is parallel to the call to Gideon. However, as pointed out before in the Samson story, this call appears before he was born, which is also mentioned in the Jeremiah story (Jer 1). Hence, from this juncture, the reader is left with two major questions: Will Samson follow his Nazarite vows? Will he deliver Israel from the Philistine oppression?

Evidently, the fact that the heavenly messenger appeared to his wife and not to him made Manoah resentful. Josephus maintained that it was jealousy that played a role in the story.

> The woman when her husband arrived, reported what she heard from the angel, extolling the young man's comeliness and stature in such wise that he in his jealousy was driven by these praises to distraction and to conceive the suspicions that such passion arouses. But she wishing to ally her husband's unreasonable distress, entreated God to send the angel again that her husband also might see him.[22]

According to Josephus, Manoah suspected his wife of adultery with a stranger. Therefore, she prayed that the messenger would appear to her husband and convince him of her innocence. According to this version, the narrator, the listeners, and the readers were aware that something happened between the visitor and Manoah's wife.[23]

Evidently, Manoah did not trust his wife, so he did not believe her message. Manoah prayed to God and pleaded with Him to send the divine messenger again. To conceal his true motivation, he said so that the man can teach him and his wife how to bring up the boy who is to be born. More so, he did not ask for new instructions, he wanted to hear for himself the message that his wife received because he wanted to authenticate it. We have to remember that his wife said that she did not know who the man was or from where he came. Thus, it makes sense to ask that the man reappear and deliver his message. Appearing twice and delivering the message would

---

21. Asis, "Significance of the Narrative," 25.
22. Josephus, *Ant.* 5.279–80.
23. Margalith, "More Samson Legends," 401.

serve as a sign that it is indeed a message from God. Interestingly, this is the only place in the Hebrew Bible where an angel returns and appears for a second time.

The Angel's Second Appearance

God responded to Manoah's plea and sent the messenger back to earth. Previously the messenger did not appear to Manoah, but he appeared first to his wife. Apparently, Manoah and his wife were not together at the time. The narrator tells the reader that she was out in the field. The field is usually an open place in uninhabited country far from human homes. In the Hebrew Bible, it is often a place of crime. In the field, Cain killed his brother Abel (Gen 3:8). The woman from Tekoa had two sons and one killed the other (2Sam 14:6). In the field, if the body of a slain person is found, the community needs to slaughter a heifer in a wadi and wash their hands over the heifer and declare their innocence (Deut 21:1–9). The Book of Deuteronomy deals with a case of an engaged woman who is attacked in the field by a man who laid with her. The man's punishment for his crime is death, while the girl does not incur the death penalty because she cried for help and there was no one to save her (22:25–27). The fact that this meeting between Manoah's wife and the messenger took place in the field and that "Manoah was not with her" (Judg 13:9) might raise the suspicion that something happened between the women and the messenger. Brettler suggests that the Hebrew "come to" can indicate a sexual relationship, and the man of God is the father of the boy.[24] Guillaume also points to the lack of the usual formula: "He knew or entered his wife and she conceived."[25] But the lack of the formula does not prove the Manoah is not the father, and as Zakovitz pointed out already, the use of "come to" simply refers to his appearance to her and no more.[26]

Upon recognizing the man, she runs to her husband to inform him about the man who spoke to her earlier. The couple returned to the field and found the man. Manoah followed his wife because she knew the place where the messenger was to be found. According to Abravanel, Manoah was suspicious about the person who appeared alone to his wife, and more so, he was also afraid that person might harm his wife. The fact that

---

24. Brettler, *Judges*, 45.
25. Guillaume, *Waiting for Josiah*, 166.
26. Zakovitz, *Life of Samson*, 46.

Manoah was suspicious can be surmised from the question he posed to the man: "Are you the one who talked to my wife?" (v.11). To this question, the man answered with one Hebrew word, "I am." With a series of questions, Manoah tried to extract information from the man. He wanted to know when the messenger's words would be fulfilled and what is to be the rule for the boy's life and work. In other words, he wanted to know the destiny of his son. According to *Numbers Rabbah*, he asked how the child should conduct himself after birth and what the mother should do until the day of his birth.[27]

The messenger did not respond to Manoah at all. Instead, he repeated his previous message. His wife must do what she was told before. The visitor added only a small detail of information; Manoah's wife should avoid consumption of any grape products, not just wine. By repeating the instruction to Manoah, the messenger insinuated that it is now his responsibility to make sure that the child's Nazirite status is protected from birth.

As noted previously, this story is similar to Genesis 18 and Judges 6:17–24 where a meal is offered to a heavenly visitor. In Genesis, a meal is offered first, and then the parents received the news of the birth of their son. In our story, they received the news first, and then a meal is offered. In Genesis, the heavenly visitors agreed to eat, while in our story, the guest refused. In the Gideon story, on the other hand, the offering of a meal was because Gideon wanted to know if the words of the messenger would come true and he would defeat the Midianites (6:16–18). It appears that the offering of a meal to heavenly visitors has one purpose, which is to receive a divine blessing.

Manoah offered to prepare a kid for the messenger. Similarly, Gideon offered to the angel a kid (6:19); Jesse sent a present to King Saul that included a kid (1Sam16:20); Judah sent a kid to redeem the pledge from Tamar (Gen 38:17); and Samson tried to appease his wife by bringing a kid as a present (Judg 15:1). Evidently, serving and offering a kid was as a form of tribute. On the other hand, when Samson tore the lion, he did so with bare hands as one might tear a kid.

The messenger refused to eat the food that was offered to him by Manoah. Instead, he suggested that the proper gesture is to prepare a burnt offering and offer it to the Lord. By this, he is hinting to his identity. Why he refused to eat we are not told. According to the Talmud, when a meal is

---

27. *Num. R. 10.*

offered, one has to conform to the local custom and eat (Gen 18:8).[28] Still, the messenger refused to eat because it was not offered as hospitality to strangers but as gratitude for good news. What is strange here is that even at this stage, Manoah still is not aware that the person he is speaking with is a messenger of Yahweh. Therefore, not surprisingly, he asks for the identity of the stranger, asking for his name.

The pursuit for the deity's name is a well-known motif that already is found in the Jacob cycle. Jacob asked his mysterious assailant to reveal his name (Gen 32:22–32); Moses asked God to reveal his name (Exod 3:13); and Pharaoh asked: "Who is the Lord that I should heed Him and let Israel go" (5:2). It was believed that knowing the name gives power over the name. Possessing no name means nonexistence: name giving was associated with domination, for the person who gives the name has power over the object. Hence, Adam gave names to all the wild beasts and all the birds in the sky (Gen 2:19). The messenger's response to Manoah's inquiry, "You must not ask for my name," (Judg 13:18) is similar to the answer Jacob received from the mysterious assailant (Gen 32:30). The stories in Judges and in Genesis show that any attempt to discover the identity of the divine being is turned aside. We have to remember that in the pre-exilic period, all the angels remain anonymous and are nameless. More so, in our story, the messenger says that his name is unknowable. As a matter of fact, he does not reveal his name but tries to give an explanation to the meaning of his name. He uses the Hebrew word פלאי *pel'î* to describe the meaning of his name, which means miraculous. The term is connected with the cognate noun פלא *pele'*, which refers to God's miraculous acts of judgment and salvation. In other words, the messenger refers to the fact that the future birth of the boy to a barren woman is the result of God's doing.

Rashi (Rabbi Solomon ben Isaac 1040–1105) based on *Genesis Rabbah*, explains the word פלאי *pel'î* is constantly changing and it is not known to what it was changed to today.[29] *Numbers Rabbah* 10 explains that the angels had temporary names based on their wondrous mission. According to the Midrash, the angel said to himself that he will never see Manoah again, therefore, there is no need to inquire about his name.

Manoah followed the messenger's counsel and offered the kid and a meal offering to the Lord. Manoah added here the meal offering, which is not mentioned in his original suggestion (Judg 13:15). In contrast, Gideon

28. b. B. Meṣ. 86b.
29. Gen. R. 78.

first offered the meal offering (6:18), and then added to it the kid (v. 19). In the Gideon story, the offering consisted of baked unleavened bread from an איפה *'êpâ* and flour (ibid), which is mentioned many times in the Torah and in the prophetic books as part of a meal offering מנחה *minḥah*. In our story, the sacrifice is termed as *minḥah*, but since איפה *'êpâ* and flour were part of it, it was not necessary to mention it. Like Gideon, Manoah offered the sacrifice on the rock. It is noteworthy that in the Gideon story, the messenger of Yahweh performs a miracle *pele'* פלא and sets the offering on fire and he disappears in flames. Describing the angel's action, the narrator uses wordplay here. He employs the root פלא p. l.' which in the Samson story described the unknowable name of the messenger. The fire that is mentioned leaped toward the sky. Fire that reaches so high is usually mentioned with the burning of complete cities (Josh 8:20; Judg 20:40). In our story, it is a heavenly fire, however, it does not come from heaven but goes up. (Lev 10:1). All this time Manoah and his wife were watching as the events unfolded before their eyes. At this stage, they realized that it was the angel of God who appeared and spoke with them. Thus, they fell on their faces in submission and out of awe. The narrator adds that the angel never again appeared to Manoah and his wife and tells the reader that Manoah realized that it was indeed an angel of the Lord.

Realizing that they saw an angel of God, Manoah, like Gideon (Judg 6:22), expects that he and his wife will die. Jacob after his encounter with the mysterious assailant said: "I have seen a divine being face to face, yet my life has been preserved" (Gen 33: 31). Moses at the burning bush hid his face, "for he was afraid to look at God" (Exod 3:6). In the Hebrew Bible, we read of the encounter between humans and God. Humans were afraid of the divine manifestation, as these encounters were a terrifying experience full of dread. Because of this, God became more remote and appeared to humans in the form of dreams in order to mitigate the shock of the theophany. When Moses asked God: "Oh, let me behold Your Presence!" (33:18), God's answer to Moses is: "But He said, you cannot see My face, for a man may not see Me and live" (v.20).

Following the angel's disappearance, Manoah's wife enters the scene. She was in the background the whole time while her husband spoke with the messenger. She did not ask any questions. She remains silent she is portrayed as cool and calculating. In contrast to her husband, she understood that the angel is only a messenger, and therefore, there is no threat to their lives. Her husband stresses the fact that they saw God, while she stresses

The Birth of Samson

the hearing element. They heard the message that was sent to them by God. Hence, they will not die; God does not want to kill them. It was God who wanted them to see the angel; it was not an accident that they saw the angel. More so, if God wanted to kill them, He would not accept their tribute that they had presented to him. O'Connell points out that in the Gideon story, when the angel told Gideon that he would not die, Gideon understood the significance of the theophany, and therefore, built an altar to God. Not so with Manoah, although he also realized in the end that he met an angel and he would not die, he did not build an altar to God.[30] This comparison evidently diminishes from Manoah's image, which is overshadowed by his wife throughout the whole chapter.

With the ending of the revelation, the narrator quickly informs the reader that the woman gave birth to a boy naming him Samson, he grew and God blessed him. Many times in the biblical narrative, the narrative is very laconic and very economical in its descriptions; only important details and events are described. The years from his birth to his youth are skipped with no description given. We read that he was born, and then "the boy grew" (Judg 13:24). This is prevalent in the biblical narrative, hence, in the story of the birth of Jacob and Esau, the narrator mentions several details that will impact the relations between the brothers (Gen 25: 24–26), but immediately he describes them in their youth: "When the boys grew up, Esau became a skillful hunter, a man of outdoor; but Jacob was a mild man who stayed in camp," (v.27). Moses was educated and spent many years in Pharaoh's court, however, not a single word is mentioned. First we read that Pharaoh's daughter gave him his name and next we read that he acted on behalf of his brothers: "Sometime after that, when Moses had grown up, he went out to his kinsfolk and witnessed their labor" (Exod 2:11).

Skipping the description of the early years of Samson caused Josephus to describe the boy as growing fast.[31] In addition to mentioning that he grew, we read that God blessed him. This also appears in the story about Ishmael where we read: "God was with the boy and he grew up" (Gen 21:20). And in the Samuel story: "Samuel grew up and the Lord was with him" (1Sam 3:19). In other words, God was with Samson, which guarantees his success.

In birth announcements, it is God who usually gives the child's name with an explanation. Not so here, as Samson's mother gives him his name, which is possibly because she was first informed about his birth. More so,

---

30. O'Connell, *Rhetoric*, 218.
31. Joseph, *Ant.* 5.8:4.

she is the one who spoke initially to the angel. Generally speaking, examination of name-giving in the Bible shows that half were given by the father and half by the mother. What is strange here is that there is no explanation of the name. Usually we find a midrashic explanation to biblical names such as with Isaac, Jacob, Moses, Samuel, and many others. It appears as though the narrator avoided explaining the name for fear of the connection between the name Samson and mythological elements. The Hebrew name Samson is from the Hebrew root שמש *šmš*, which means sun. Not clear, however, is the ending of the name with the suffix *ōn*, which might be understood as diminutive, hence, "suns child" or "solar" sunny or "suns man." It is possible that the ending *ōn* comes from the Ugaritic *yanu*, which is found in Ugaritic personal names. Interestingly, the name *shmsn* occurs as a Syrian place name.[32]

The sun deity was well-known in the Ancient Near East. The Hittites worshiped a god and a goddess of the sun. Philo of Byblos mentioned that the first settlers in Phoenicia, Aeon, and Protogonos would raise their hands toward the sun during a drought, since they considered him the Lord of the sky and they called him Beelsamen.[33] Uta was the Sumerian name or the Semitic Shamash, the sun, which was the god of justice and was worshipped at the temple of Ebabbar in Sippar in northern Babylonia. The cult of the sun was very popular in Palestine; this is evident from names such as Beth-Shemesh, En-Shemesh, and Ir-Shemesh. Still, it was forbidden in Deuteronomy 4:19 and 17:3, which is the only book of the Torah to mention such practices. (See chapter 6 for more on sun worship.)

Not surprisingly, Josephus tried to reject the connection between the name Samson with the sun deity, therefore, he explains the name from שמן *shāmān* "robust," in other words strong, "and they called the child, when he was born, Samson, which name signifies one that is strong."[34] The sages followed a similar path and explained that the sun is an epithet of God based on the biblical verse:

> "R. Johanan said Samson was called by the name of the Holy One, blessed He; as it is said, *For the Lord God is a sun and a shield* (Ps. 84:12). According to argument, [his name] may not be erased!— The intention is that [his name] was typical of the name of the

---

32. Kraft, "Samson," In *IDB* 4:198.
33. Attridge and Oden, *Philo of Byblos*, 41.
34. Josephus, *Ant.* 5.8:4.

The Birth of Samson

Holy blessed be He; as the Holy one blessed be He, shields the world, so Samson shielded Israel during his generation."[35]

Abravanel has a different explanation: Samson devoted his life of being a servant (שָׁמָשׁ *samās*) of God. His name also referred to שְׁמָמָה *shᵉmāmâ*, desolation that he would inflict on the Philistines. Because of this, the Bible did not explain the reasons for his name so as to not alert the Philistines.

Modern scholars, on the other hand, pointed out that the name Samson appears to be connected to the Canaanite sun god Shemesh. More so, his birthplace was across the valley of Sorek, which is close to the city Beth-Shemesh "house of the sun," the site of a shrine of the sun god. The blinding of Samson is comparable to a solar eclipse. The motif of fire appears several times in the narrative, which strengthens the premise of a solar mythology. Furthermore, the story where Samson tied foxes to torches recalls the Roman festival of Cerealia, which served as a mildew-prevention technique throughout the fields.[36] These factors contributed to the belief that Samson originally was the hero of a sun myth. Although some of the elements may have been inspired by mythological heroic tales, the overall picture that emerges is about an earthly hero that had folk tales attributed to him. Samson was human and fought against the foreign oppressor.

The Purpose of the Story

Samson's stories portrayed life in Shephelah on the border between Judah, Dan, and Philistia during the late twelfth- or early eleventh-century BCE before the tribe of Dan migrated to the north. This is the beginning of the Philistines' oppression of Israel, as it is reflected in the narrative that ultimately would take place during the time of King Saul. In this period, there is still interaction between the two sides, and Samson is frequently coming and going between the two camps. The fact that there was contact between the two sides is also evident from the fact that numerous Philistine artifacts were found in the excavation of the Israelite settlement at Beth-Shemesh from that period. Israel is still not engaged in full-scale aggression with the Philistines, so we don't have any descriptions of armies fighting against each other like in later periods. Indeed, Samson is not leading an army against the Philistines when he saved Israel from the Philistines, he fights his battle alone.

---

35. b. Soṭah. 10a.
36. Crenshaw, "Samson," In *ABD* 5:590; idem, *Samson*, 16.

With Samson's birth, God gave him superhuman strength. This superhuman strength made him the arch enemy of the Philistines. He defeated them in each encounter single-handedly, and they feared him. It was inconceivable for them that any human could be so strong. Hence, they likely believed that Samson was the son of a mortal woman and a god. These types of stories were prevalent in the mythical world, which contained legends dealing with the birth of heroes. Samson's extraordinary strength led to the comparison with Greek legends like Hercules and Orion. It was suggested that the Israelites, through their ties with the Philistines who originally came from the Aegean, also became familiar with the Greek legends.[37] The myths by nature accepted polytheism, which was not accepted in ancient Israel. Hence, according to Bentzen: "The religious history of Israel is in some respect a history of 'de-mythologization'"[38] Therefore, what we have in the Hebrew Bible is only remnants and adaptations of mythological material.

In the ancient world, various myths about sexual relations between gods and daughters of men were prevalent. As a result of these unions, the children who were born were half gods or were raised to the status of deities. The Ugaritic poem, *the pleasant and beautiful gods*, describes such unions. Accordingly, El married daughters of men and had two sons šḥr and šlm who became divinities. The Hebrew Bible comes to deal with such myths and concepts. The Bible mentions stories about giants who lived upon the earth and men who had great strength. Close to the world of myth is a story in Genesis 6:1–4, where divine beings cohabit with the daughters of men who bore them offspring. Out of this union, the heroes of the old Nephilim are born. In the Book of Numbers 13:3, the Nephilim are endowed with extraordinary physical strength. The term is understood to mean giants or heroes.

The purpose of the story in Genesis was to counter the pagan legends and to minimize their traditions about giants and heroes. The biblical narrator diminished the myth by asserting that it was בני האלהים *benē hā' ĕlōhīm* who cohabitated with the daughters of men and gods. The text did not use the word for angels that refers to high-ranking angels, which represent the glory of God. Instead, it used the term *benē hā' ĕlōhīm*, which included angels of the degraded type.[39] Additionally, their decedents did

---

37. Margalith, "Legends of Samson/Heracles," 63–70.
38. Bentzen, *Introduction to the Old Testament*, 241.
39. Cassuto, *Genesis*, 1:294.

not become gods, and they did not ascend to heaven; they stayed on earth. They were like humans but with more strength and size. The story served as a polemic against the mythical traditions that described cohabitation between gods and humans. In those myths, the progeny turned out to be gods.[40] As Skinner noted: "The few passages where the old heathen conceptions of godhead still appears (1:26; 3:22, 24; 6:1ff; 11:1ff) they only serve to show how completely the religious beliefs of Israel has transformed and purified the crude speculations of pagan theology, and adapted them to the ideas of an ethical and monotheistic faith."[41] Similarly, the Samson story gives us an answer about the origin of this superhuman being. Samson is not a son of God, and his father and mother are both humans who received a divine message about the birth of their son.

Conclusion

Unlike any other judge, Samson is appointed even before his birth to deliver Israel. No explanation is given for his election. The angel of the Lord appeared to his mother and informed her that she would have a son. In addition to his declaration, the messenger also imposed restrictions on her to not drink any wine or any intoxicating beverage and also not to eat unclean food. All of this is because her future son would be a Nazirite for God from the womb. Manoah, Samson's father, did not trust his wife and did not believe her message. Hence, he prayed to God and pleaded with Him to send the divine messenger again. Responding to Manoah, God sent the messenger for a second time. In spite of Manoah's questions about what is to be the destiny of his son, the messenger did not respond to Manoah at all. Instead, he repeated his previous message. By doing so, he insinuated that it is now Manoah's responsibility to make sure that the child's Nazirite status is protected from birth. Through the whole encounter, Manoah is not aware that the person he is speaking with is a messenger of Yahweh. It is only when the angel of the Lord ascended in the flames from the altar that Manoah understood with whom he was speaking. Manoah is overshadowed by his wife through the whole chapter. She understood what they had witnessed and that the angel was only a messenger, and therefore, was no threat to their lives. It was inconceivable that a human being like Samson could be so strong. Stories of a son of a mortal woman and son of god were

40. Zakovitz, *life of Samson*, 75.
41. Skinner, *Genesis*, ix.

prevalent in the mythical world, which contained legends dealing with the birth of heroes. In the Hebrew Bible, the mythical element in which the boy became divine disappeared. Hence, our story about Samson comes to give us an answer about the origin of this superhuman being. Samson is not a son of God, and his father and mother are both humans who received a divine message about the birth of their son. The message that the narrator conveys is that the birth of Samson and the description of his battle through his life is polemic against the world of myth.

Samson's parents were told that their son would be a Nazarite starting from the womb, therefore, in the next chapter we will examine the subject of his Nazarite status and the Nazarite subject in the Hebrew Bible.

2

Nazirite

In the Hebrew Bible, a Nazir was a person who vowed to restrict himself in several areas to attain a higher measure of holiness. The Bible mentions two kinds of Nazirites, lifelong and temporary; both are the result of a vow. In the case of a lifelong Nazirite, the vow is taken by another person typically by the pregnant mother. The vow of the temporary Nazirite is self-imposed. The lifelong Nazirite was spontaneous, and it was later regulated by law so that every person who made a vow should follow a certain pattern of conduct, then he could become a Nazirite for a specific time. The Bible mentions two lifelong Nazirites: Samson and Samuel. Both were dedicated as such from the time of their conception. Hence, Samuel's mother made a pledge to devote her son to the Lord as a Nazirite even before she became pregnant. She did so hoping that God would bless her with progeny, which indeed was the case. On the other hand, Samson's mother, who was also barren, was told by the angel that she would have a son and he would be a lifelong Nazirite. In this chapter, we will examine the nature of Samson's and Samuel's Nazirite makings in light of the biblical law concerning Nazirites. We will also survey the subject of Nazirites in the Hebrew Bible.

Law of the Nazirite

The laws concerning Nazirites are found in the Book of Numbers (6:3–8). The law contains three provisions:

1. Abstain from any product of vine.
2. Allow the hair on his head to grow untrimmed.
3. Avoid contact with a corpse.

A temporary Nazirite was forbidden from drinking wine. But questions need to be raised. For one thing what is the exact meaning of the word 'wine'? It is believed that the term wine includes three components: 1. Wine that has turned sour, 2. Grapes whether fresh or dried, 3. Seeds and skin of the grape. The prohibition of any other intoxicant that is referred to as שכר *shekkar* is also mentioned. In the Hebrew Bible, this term has the meaning of any intoxicant that is not made from grapes. Indeed, we find that intoxicant drinks were made from pomegranates and dates in Ancient Egypt and Mesopotamia. In the ancient world, beer was made from barley. In Akkadian, the exact cognate *šikru, šikaru* means beer. Thus, the precise meaning of *shekkar* is not clear, and it is possible that it refers to two types of drinks since both were widespread. Albright pointed out that included among the Philistine pottery that was discovered was a jug with a strainer spout. This strained the beer of its barley husks.[1] It appears that the Philistines were particularly fond of beer. Although the Bible does not mentioned beer specifically, nevertheless, the Philistines used to have banquets that involved drinking feasts that are mentioned several times (Judg 14:10, 12, 17; 16:23, 25).

The second provision for the Nazirite was to allow his hair to grow untrimmed (Num 6:5). The uncut hair of the Nazirite is his distinctive trait; it is a visible sign of his holiness. Men regularly trim or shave their hair normally. Not so for the lifelong Nazirite, who allowed his hair to grow because he never cut it. The prohibition against cutting the hair is the most significant nazirite law. Sacredness is associated with the length of the hair. The hair must be kept from all contamination during the period of consecration. Contact with impurity required the shaving and sanctifying of the hair and then the period of consecration is over. The significance of the hair is evident in the ceremony that ends the Nazirite period. Shaving the hair is

---

1. Albright, "Some Canaanite-Phoenician sources," 10–11; idem, *Archaeology of Palestine*, 115.

the main thing (Num 6:9, 18); when the Nazirite period is completed, the Nazirite shaves his hair in front of the tent meeting. He takes his shaved hair and places it on an altar of fire (6:18).

Hair continues to grow throughout life and also for a time after death. Hence, it was considered by the ancients as the seat of man's vitality and life. Therefore, it was used in rituals. Like blood, hair symbolized the life of a person. Hair offering was common in the worship of the gods. The hair of Achilles was dedicated to the river god Spercheus so he would return safe to Troy. But knowing that he would not return, the offering was made to the dead Patroclus.[2] Similarly, the heathen Arabs cut off their hair and placed it on the tomb to create a connection between the living and the dead.[3] It is noteworthy, that even today at the dawn of the twenty-first century many Israelis make a pilgrimage to the tomb of Rabbi Simeon Bar Yochai near Safed, where they cut the hair of their children for the first time and leave it there.

In the ancient world, it was believed that the offering of the hair came to form a bond between the living and their god. A testimony to this practice appears in a Phoenician inscription from Kition in Cyprus that dates to the ninth-century BCE. The inscription was found in the temple on a bowl with writing on its outside surface, indicating that it contained the hair of the donor. It mentions hair that was shaved and dedicated to the goddess in exchange of petitionary vow.[4]

The offering of hair is also found in later times in Babylonia, Syria (Lucian), Greece, and Arabia. There is a particular testimony by Lucian, which is most telling:

> "The young men make an offering of their beards, while the young women let their 'sacred locks' grow from birth and when they finally come to the temple, they cut them. When they have placed them in containers, some of silver and many of gold, they nail them up to the temple, and they depart after each inscribes his name. When I was still a youth I too, preformed this ceremony and even now my locks and name are in the sanctuary."[5]

Milgrom makes an analogy to the Absalom story by suggesting that he offered his hair. According to the Hebrew Bible, Absalom cut his hair

---

2. Robertson Smith, *Lectures on Religion*, 325.
3. Cook, *Ezekiel*, 485.
4 Dupont -Sommer , A. "Une Inscription phénicienne," 2–28.
5. Lucian, *De Dea Syria*, 60.

The Samson Story

מקץ ימים לימים *mikkets yamim la-yamim* (2Sam 14:26). Hence, if the phrase is rendered "annually at the yearly feast," then it is possible that Absalom offered his hair on the sanctuary.[6] Similarly, the Rabbis suggested:

> "It has been taught: Rabbi said that Absalom was life—nazirite, for it says, *And it came to pass at the end of forty years that Absalom said to the king: I pray thee, let me go and pay my vow which I have vowed unto the Lord in Hebron.* He used to cut his hair every twelve months, for it says, [*And when he polled his head*] *now it was at every year's [yamim] end [that he polled it]*."[7]

The fact that Absalom vowed to serve the Lord and that the Bible mentioned the length of his hair leads to the conclusion that he was a lifelong Nazirite. However, in the stories about Absalom, there is no connection between his hair (2Sam 14:25–26) and the vow he took at Geshur (15:8). More so, there are no Nazirite elements in the vow he took at Hebron (15:7). The hair and the vow are integral parts of the story, and serve as a background to the story. However, there is no connection between them. The vow was the reason why Absalom went to Hebron, while his hair describes his beauty and also plays a role in his death.

The third prohibition is about coming into contact with a corpse. The sanctity of Nazirites is so extreme that they are subject to a ban of defiling themselves for the dead, which is equal to the stringency applied to the high priest (Num 6:6–7). Nowhere is it stipulated how the Nazirite should conduct himself with regard to other forms of ritual impurity, but the stringencies imposed regarding the impurity of the dead apparently brought with them a whole series of rules of conduct concerning many other forms of impurity. The impurity of death is the most extreme form of defilement (Lev 5:2; 6:9; 9:6–7). Anthropologists say that primitive human beings believed that corpses were impure and must be avoided. The taboo was motivated by fear of death. According to Frazer, fear of the dead is a key element of primitive religion. Mourners wore special garments to keep the spirits from identifying them. Another fear was of the disease-causing infection that might be contracted from the dead.[8] Eichrodt emphasized the element of fear. He says that the Israelites' mourning customs, such as rending their garments, dressing in sackcloth, and spreading ashes on their

---

6. Milgrom, *Numbers*, 357.
7. b. Naz. 4b.
8. Frazer, *Fear of the Dead*, 11.

head were all part of "an attempt to make oneself unrecognizable to the dead for the fear of their envy or malice."[9]

Whereas, others are defiled only by direct contact with a corpse or by being under the same roof with it; the Nazirite and high priest are defiled even by their proximity to a dead body. Milgrom cites examples from the ancient world of situations in which a person could be defiled by sight and not by contact.[10] According to Lucian (second century), in Syria, priests who merely saw a corpse had to purify themselves in a special ceremony and were not allowed to enter their temple until the next day.[11] In ancient Greece, a person who saw a corpse was not allowed to enter a temple. Some Mesopotamian texts state that people (not just priests) contracted impurities when they saw a corpse.[12]

When a Nazirite becomes impure or when someone dies unexpectedly, the Bible specifies what they must do. In this case, the Nazirite vow, symbolized by long hair, is invalidated by the pollution. The Nazirite is impure for seven days, after which he or she must undergo rites of purification like any other person defiled by a dead body. The long hair, no longer consecrated, must be cut off. According to the Mishnah, the hair must be buried to prevent it from defiling other objects.[13] The head is shaved as a sign that the vow has been breached. This action is performed on the seventh day because that is the last day of impurity for all those defiled by the dead.

Nazirites who were exposed to a corpse also had to bring sacrifices like anyone who sinned inadvertently. The offering consisted of a dove as a burnt offering, a dove as a sin offering, and, after an interval of time, a ram as a guilt offering. During this interval, Nazirites reconsecrated their hair and vow. In no other case does the Bible prescribe a waiting period between the required sacrifices. Why must the vow be renewed before the guilt offering is brought? In all cases of a guilt offering, the transgressor must repay the sanctuary for profaning the sacred before a sacrifice can be brought for atonement (Lev 5:14–16). That is, the holy object must be restored before the Lord will forgive the sin. The same thing applies to a Nazirite who has been defiled. The guilt offering was not acceptable until the Nazirite restores the status quo ante—the

---

9. Eichrodt, *Theology of the Old Testament*, 2:215.
10. Milgrom, *Numbers*, 46, no. 16
11. Lucian, *De Dea Syria*, 57, no. 53.
12. Milgrom, *Numbers*, 304, no. 16.
13. *m. Temurah.* 7:4.

hair that was shaved off and the period of the vow that was interrupted. Only then could the priest bring the Nazirite's guilt offering to the altar, in the hope that he or she will be forgiven.[14]

The proscriptions of drinking wine and coming into contact with the dead resemble those that apply to priests; those incumbent on the Nazirite are much stricter. A priest, for example, may not partake of strong drink when he enters the sanctuary (Lev 10:9; Ezek 44:21), but is permitted to do so outside its precincts (Isa 28:7); and there is certainly no ban on other products of the vine. As for defilement by the dead, here the Nazirite resembles the high priest, who is not even allowed to approach the corpses of his nearest relatives. Priests, too, are not allowed to shave their heads, but on the other hand, they are not allowed to let it grow long and must consequently clip it frequently (Ezek 44:20)

Samson in Light of the Biblical Law

What we read about Samson and Samuel does not correspond to the laws in Numbers 6 that we have discussed thus far. The restrictions that were imposed on them are not the same as those mentioned in the Book of Numbers. The prohibition of not drinking wine or other intoxicating beverages nor eating any product of the vine was given to Samson's mother (Judg 13:4, 7, 14). But there is not a single word regarding Samson. However, some have argued that the restrictions should be understood as relating to Samson as well. Blenkinsopp suggested that the Samson narrative is arranged around the theme of how Samson broke his vow.[15] The Bible mentions that he went into the Timnah vineyard and it is suggested that he drank at his marriage feast (14:5, 10). But this does not prove anything. It is more likely that he simply followed the restrictions that were imposed on his mother. As for the marriage feast, "Samson made a feast there, as young men used to do," Milgrom pointed out that this indicates that Samson was reluctant to play the host.[16] But he still takes part in it, which points to the fact the he might have been drinking.

There were different degrees of contamination, but the most severe one is contamination by a corpse, which was considered a major violation of the Nazirite law. Samson ate the honey from the carcasses of the lion

---

14. Milgrom, *Numbers*, 47.
15. Blenkinsopp, "Structure Style in Judges 13–16," 65–76.
16. Milgrom, *Numbers*, 356.

(14:9), killed 30 men in Ashkelon (14:19) and also stripped them of their clothing. He also killed 1,000 Philistines with the jawbone of an ass (15:15). Killing people in war time was probably the exception to the rule. More so, corpse contamination is not mentioned among the restrictions on Samson. The restriction that his mother received was not to "eat anything unclean" (Judg 13:14). According to Licht, the connection between Samson's mother's restrictions and the Nazirite law is not clear.[17] He also does not see any difficulties in the fact that Samson ate honey from the carcass of a lion since we don't know the rule about honey.

The instructions that were given to Samson's mother indicates nothing about contracting impurities from the dead, which according to the Priestly code would have defiled her embryo. Hence, it appears that the lifelong Nazirite situation is similar to that of the priest. In other words when a priest is contaminated by a corpse, his priesthood is only suspended for a prescribed period of impurity and not canceled. Still, the Rabbis acknowledged that there is a difference between a Nazirite like Samson and lifelong Nazirite. According to the Mishnah: "A Life Nazirite...Whilst should he be ritually defiled, He must offer the sacrifice [prescribed] for defilement. The Nazirite like Samson . . . and if [ritually] defiled, does not offer the sacrifice [prescribed] for defilement."[18]

Chapters 14–16:16 of the Samson story do not give us a hint that Samson was a Nazirite. There is no mention of any restrictions that were imposed on Samson directly, not even a reference to his special hair. If the reader did not read the story of his birth, he would not suspect that Samson was a Nazirite. Indeed, Samson's Nazirite status is found only in the birth narrative (13:5, 7) and at the end of the story (16:17). The Nazirite law was imposed on Samson and his mother. Samson was a lifelong Nazirite and this was expressed by his hair. His mother's Nazirite rank was characterized by the prohibition to not drink wine or other intoxicating beverages nor eat any product of the vine. Samson violates the third restriction by allowing his hair to be cut (16:17ff). This is a turning point. Although, Samson broke his first two restrictions, God was with him. He still could call on God at times of distress (15:18). He ate from the carcasses of the lion and probably drank wine. God was with Samson as long as he kept the third prohibition. Evidently, this was the most crucial element and served as a sign of Nazirite

---

17. Licht, *Numbers (1–10)*, 85.
18. b. Naz. 4b.

status. Nevertheless, when Samson falls into the hands of the Philistines, he turns once more to God who allows him to fulfill his death wish.

Interestingly, the text is silent about Samson breaking the Nazirite vow. There is no explicit condemnation of Samson's actions. More so, it seems that Yahweh was behind Samson's behavior (14:4, 19; 15:14–15).[19] It is strange that the fidelity to the Nazirite vow, which seems to be a central issue in the story, appears only in two places (13:15; 16:17), and apart from these there is no demand for obedience. More so, there is no warning regarding the significance of his disobedience. This led scholars to believe that chapter 13 had an independent origin. In other words, chapters 14–15 were originally independent from chapter 13 and they contain an older Samson story. Von Rad, for example, viewed the addition of chapter 13 as significant. He suggested that the Samson story served as a negative example to Israel. According to him, the stories about Samson and Saul and Samuel show the failure of a charismatic leader when divine powers are wasted.[20] Exum offered a different view that the Nazarite should not play a primary role in the interpretation of the Samson story. What's developed through the narrative is the focus on prayer and the deity response to prayer.[21] Examination of the narrative shows that the narrator does not assess Samson negatively. His deeds appear neutral and should be viewed according to their context in the narrative. Chapter 13 serves as an introduction to the main characters of the Samson story. Samson is introduced as a Nazarite, and the text says that his hair should not be cut. If we omit chapter 13 from the cycle, we are left with many open questions such as the source of Samson's physical strength and the significance of his hair. Without chapter 13, the various pieces of the puzzle do not fit.

Samuel in Light of the Biblical Law

As part of her vow, Hannah declared "no razor shall ever touch his head" (1Sam 1:11). This is Hannah's only restriction that is connected to the laws of the Nazirite. Still, the Book of Samuel is silent about this subject, and there is not a single word about Samuel cutting his hair or not. The other prohibition against drinking wine or other intoxicating beverages, nor to eat any product of the vine, is not mentioned in the Samuel story. Not

19. Exum, "Theological Dimension," 31.
20. Von Rad, *Old Testament Theology*, 1:334.
21. Exum, "Theological Dimension," 33.

surprisingly, Samuel took part in a feast (9:19), which indicates that probably there was some kind of intoxicant. Corpse contamination, which was part of the Nazirite law, is also not mentioned. Like Samson, Samuel also could not stay away from contact with dead bodies, for he slayed Agag in pieces (15:33). Josephus, on the other hand, says that Samuel did not kill Agag but gave the order to kill him.[22] Reading the stories about Samuel shows that there is no evidence that Samuel acted as a Nazirite, on the contrary, Samuel is acting as a priest, prophet, and a judge, never as a Nazirite. Samuel is also mentioned in Psalms 99:6, but as "among those who call on His name—when they called to the Lord." Here, the Psalmist mentions Samuel along with Moses and Aaron as people who God gave his people as priests, mediators and intercessors that they would establish relationship between God and his people. As Moses and Aaron interceded on behalf of their people, so did Samuel. It is probably the similarities "no razor shall ever touch his head," which exists in the Samson and Samuel stories, that led to the assumption that Samuel is also Nazarite, however, this was not the case.

The question of Samuel's Nazirite status occupied also the Talmudic sages. Hence, in the Talmud we find different opinions about Samuel Nazarite. Samuel was a Nazirite, in the opinion of R. Nehorai as it says,

> And there shall no razor [morah] came upon his head. It says with reference to Samson, and [no] razor [morah] and it says with reference to Samuel, and [no] razor [morah]; just as morah in the case of Samson [is used of] a nazirite, so [we should say] morah in the case of Samuel [is used of] a nazirite. R. Jose objected: But has no morah reference to [fear of] a human being? R. Nehorai said to him: But does it not also say, and Samuel said; 'How can I Go? If Saul hear it he will kill me' [which shows] that he was in fact afraid of human being?[23]

R. Nehorai says that Samuel was a Nazirite like Samson based the verse "no razor came upon his head," which is found in both the Samson and Samuel stories. R. Jose, on the other hand, does not accept that Samuel was Nazarite. He gives the word מורא *morah* a different interpretation where it now means fear.

---

22. Josephus. *Ant.* 6:155.
23. *b. Naz.*66a.

Samson's Mother

According to Judges 13: 7 Samson's mother was ordered not to drink wine or other intoxicants, and not to eat unclean food because her son would be a Nazirite for God from the womb. It is believed that she was a Nazirite as long as she was pregnant. We are not told when she ended her Nazirite period. Was she supposed to end it with the birth of Samson or when she ended weaning him? We usually read about people who take a vow of the Nazirite. But this is not the case with Samson's mother as she is ordered by the angel to become a Nazirite the first time the angel appears to her. Then, the second time when the angel appears, it is to her and her husband. Although she is Nazirite, there is no reference to this status in the story. As for the Nazirite restrictions, it is noteworthy that the author mentions the prohibition of drinking before eating because he is influenced by the Nazarite laws. The prohibition against eating unclean food is not mentioned in the Nazirite law. Instead the prohibition against eating certain types of creatures and animals is found in the priestly code (Lev 11:8). There, the prohibition is against eating or even touching animals. In Leviticus 17:15 and Deuteronomy 14:21 is the prohibition of eating the flesh of any animal that has died or was torn by beasts. Eating them is forbidden and touching the impure animal requires purification ablutions. This prohibition includes the whole Israelite community and was not limited to priests. Samson's mother did not touch the carcass of the lion that Samson killed, nor did she eat its flesh. She only ate the honey that was found in it. She probably maintained her Nazirite vow during her pregnancy. Again, we cannot tell when she ended her Nazarite period. Nonetheless, we have here a Nazirite for a limited period. Usually, we would expect to hear about a ceremony that ended her vow, but here there is no mention of it.

Hannah, Samuel's mother

The other famous Nazirite female that is mentioned in the Hebrew Bible is Hannah, Samuel's mother. Samson's mother's Nazirite status was not self-imposed; she was ordered by an angel to follow the laws of the Nazirite. Not so with Samuel's mother, who dedicated her son to the Lord before his birth. According to the Torah, entry into a Nazirite vow is self-commitment, but here it is Hannah who makes the decision for her son. In her vow, Hannah declares: "and if You will grant your maidservant a male child, I will dedicate him to the Lord for all the days of his life; and no razor shall ever touch his head "(1Sam 1:11). In other words, Samuel, like Samson, begins his Nazirite status from the womb. However, we should stress that in the Book of Samuel, the prophet Samuel is not called specifically Nazir. Based on 1Sam 1:11, 22, it was suggested that he was. Indeed, in text 4QSama we read: "Then I shall set him before you as a Nazirite until the day of his death."[24] An interesting version is found in Josephus: "And the woman, mindful of the vow which she had made concerning the child, delivered him to Eli, dedicating him to God to become a prophet; so his locks were left to grow and his drink was water."[25] Josephus, evidently, was familiar with a version where Samuel avoided drinking wine. Indeed, in the LXX there is an addition to 1Samuel 1:11, which Hannah adds before the hair vow: 'and wine and strong drink he will not drink.'[26] Nevertheless, Josephus still refers to him as a prophet, hence, creating consistency by calling him a prophet throughout the whole story. There is no mention in this story of any restrictions on Hannah during her pregnancy, like on Samson's mother. Samson's mother is ordered to not drink wine or other intoxicants, while in the Samuel story, Eli thought that Hannah was drunk. The only restriction that Samson and Samuel share is "and no razor come upon his head." This, as we mentioned before, led to the assumption that Samuel also was a Nazirite. Still, the Book of Samuel shows no mention of Samuel letting his hair grow, a motif which is very prevalent in Samson's description. In other words, there is no proof in the Hebrew Bible that Samuel was a Nazarite for life. Moreover, it is not clear why Hannah did not mention to Eli that "and no razor come upon his head" when she handed her son to serve in the temple in Shiloh. The custom of dedicating young boys and delivering them to serve in the temple as oblates is known from ancient Mesopotamia.[27] It usually involved women who were barren who turned to their god in prayer to conceive. In return, they promised to dedicate their son to serve their god in the temple. However, there is no mention of a temporary nor a lifelong Nazirite vow in these cases.

24. McCarter, *I Samuel*, 53.
25. Josephus, *Ant.* 5.347
26. For further study see: Tsevat, "Was Samuel a Nazirite?" 199–204.
27. Oppenheim, *Ancient Mesopotamia*, 107.

Nazir in the Bible

Genesis 49:26 and Deuteronomy 33:16 refer to Joseph as a נזיר *nazir*. However, it is possible that the Hebrew word *nazir* may refer to one who wears נזר *nēzer* which was the symbol of royal power (2Sam 1:10; 2Kgs 11:12). Indeed, the LXX, Pseudo Jonathan, Peshita and the Samaritan understood *nazir* as a ruling prince. Another interpretation is based on the root נ. ז. ר. n.z.r which indicates separation. In other words, Joseph stands apart from his brothers; he is the one who is selected for a holy life. Hence, the Vulgate and the Midrash understood it as Nazirite.[28] But it is more likely that he is elected among of his brothers because he had received his father's extraordinary blessings.

In the Song of Deborah, there is a reference to the Nazirite vow and rule against shaving one's hair. "When locks go untrimmed פרעות (*perāʿôt*) in Israel, When fighting men dedicated themselves—bless Yahweh!" (Judg 5:2). The verb פרע *pāraʿ* and its nominal reflexes may refer to the loosening of the hair to let it go untrimmed. The mention of dedication in the verse may allude to a vow. The Hebrew word עם *ʿam* can be translated as "fighting men." It is possible that we have a reference to the custom of taking a vow and letting the hair grow during the time of war. The fighting men who fought the wars of Yahweh dedicated themselves and did not shave. This is similar to Samson who was a Nazirite and was also involved in wars.

Another connection between war and the Nazirite appears in Deuteronomy 32:42 ". . . Blood of the slain and captive, From the long-haired enemy." In the ancient world, there was a practice among warriors to let their hair grow in the belief that strength resides in their hair or as a dedication to the deity. The Hebrew Bible reveals that the camp had to be holy and the warriors pure because of God's presence (Deut 23:10–14). There are suggestions that warriors maintained ritual purity and avoided sexual contact before the battle. Thus, David claimed to follow it or pretended to follow it (1Sam 21:5–6). Uriah slept at the entrance of the royal palace and did not go down to his house to maintain his purity (2Sam 11:11). The fighting men were consecrated before battle (Josh 3:5). This was, "Because the war was sacral, a sphere of activity in which Israel's God was present, the camp and the warriors had to be ritually purified."[29]

---

28. *Gen. R. 98:20*
29. Miller, *Divine Warrior*, 157.

Nazirite

Another mention of Nazirtite appears in Jeremiah 35. The Rechabites were a small religious sect who were descendants of Jonadab son of Rechab. God commanded Jeremiah to take the Rechabites to one of the chambers in the Temple and serve them wine. The Rechabites refused since they did not drink wine, as their ancestor Jonadab son of Rechab forbade them to drink wine. More so, they were not allowed to cultivate or to own fields or vineyards or to build houses. They remained tent dwellers until the invasion of Nebuchadnezzar, when they had to take refuge in Jerusalem (Jer 35:65). Their way of life was the essence of nomadic life, which is the opposite of the urban way of life. The Nabateans are similar to the Rechabites who were also forbidden to build homes or plant vines.[30] According to Gray, the reason for such restrictions was the "attempt of certain classes to maintain a more primitive way of life: the cultivation of vine. . .is one of the marked differences between the nomadic life. . . and the settled agriculture life."[31]

Amos 2:11–12 mentions the prophet and the Nazirite together and suggests high status for the Nazir. God had called both, and they were dedicated to the service of Yahweh. They are mentioned next to the prophets because, by their own voluntary ritual behavior and vows, they exemplify the will of God.[32] Their way of life is a mark of their dedication to God. Commenting on Amos 2:11–12, de Vaux says: "In this text, the Nazirite is not a person who has taken a vow, but a man possessed of a God-given charisma: it is a lifelong state resulting from a call by God."[33] God separated him from the realm of profane things. The Nazirites like the Prophets, were chosen from the womb and had a special relationship with God. Amos speaks about the people corrupting the Nazirites and then silencing the prophets. The Nazirites were forced to drink wine and forced to break their vows of abstinence. This conduct provoked God's involvement. The relationship between the Nazirite and God is intimate. The mention of Nazirites in Amos is uncommon since they are not referred to in any of the other prophetic literature. Besides Samson and Samuel, no other Nazirites are known. The mention of Nazirites and prophets together serves as a testimony of Israel failing to deal with those whom God sent to serve his people.[34]

---

30. Diod. *Sic.xix.94.3*
31. Gray, *Numbers*, 62.
32. Paul, *Amos*, 92.
33. de Vaux, *Ancient Israel*, 467.
34. Andersen and Freedman, *Amos*, 331.

Origin of Nazirite Law

A question needs to be asked as to the origin of the Nazirite law: What were the reasons for this law? One of the explanations is that it originated as a reaction against Canaanite practices. The Israelites were unable to conquer the Canaanites completely and through their contact with them they were losing their distinctive features. If they wanted to continue with their existence and be the people of Yahweh and to serve Him, they had to return to their ancient customs that were brought from the desert. This process of returning to their ancient customs and living a nomadic life started as early as the time of the Judges, and the Nazirites were the leading force of this development. Hence, we read about abstention from alcohol and growth of hair. But the Bible shows that wine was part of the Yahweh cult, libations were associated with various offerings (Exod 29:40; Num 15:5; 28:14; 1Chr 9:29) and sacrificial meals included wine (Deut 14:26). The prophets Amos and Isaiah criticized the usage of wine that was acquired through injustice.

A more likely reason for the origin of the Nazirites are their roots in a holy war.[35] As mentioned before, the fighting man took a vow and let their hair grow at the time of war. Indeed, in her victory song, Deborah refers to Nazirites' rule against shaving one's hair. More so, in the Samson story when the angel of the Lord told Manoah's wife no razor should touch his head, he also told her that he shall be the first to deliver Israel from the Philistines. In other words, Samson's task was to be a hero who would fight against the enemies and save the Israelites from oppression. He, indeed, did start to deliver the Israelites but this mission was completed by King David. Similarly, Samuel also led the Israelites in their fight against the Philistines (1Sam 7:9–14). Evidently, this connection between hair and war, coupled with the belief that the strength resided in the hair, led to the assumption that the origin of Nazir is from a holy war.

Nazirite law is found in the Book of Numbers. It is believed that the Priestly legislation is late and reflects the period after the Babylonian exile; therefore, the Nazirite laws, which are mentioned in it, are also late. In other words, until the end of the First Temple period, lifelong Nazirites were the norm and only in the later period was the temporary Nazirite status introduced. However, if the Priestly source is earlier, then the two types of Nazirites could exist side by side. Samson and Samuel are mentioned in the prophetic

---

35. Mayer, "נזר nzr," In *TDOT* 9:308.

books which dismisses the possibility that they were not aware of a temporary Nazirite status.

The temporary Nazirite became a private matter of self-discipline where the individual made a vow to God in order to receive his wishes or to escape from danger. Saying such as 'I will become a nazirite' if such and such a thing happens, became the norm. Hence, it was the scribes with their creativity who developed it into a law. Instead of a lifelong Nazirite, they shortened it to 30 days. The Nazirite became a private matter, it was initiated by the person himself, not his parents. Terminating the Nazirite status required a sacrifice, thus, it was under priestly control. The early Nazirites served the nation; they did it by the name of Yahweh because they had a mission to help their people. Not so with the temporary Nazirite vow, which was purely private. The law of the Nazirite in Numbers 6 does not mention the lifelong Nazirite. Still, two of the three prohibitions that are mentioned in the law of the Nazirites are also part of the lifelong Nazirites; not to drink wine or any product of wine and cutting the hair. The third prohibition, corpse contamination, distinguishes the temporary from the lifelong Nazirites.

The Samson story is describing the lifelong Nazirite as it contains elements from the law of Nazirite in addition to the motif of election. Samson's Nazirite status is expressed through his hair, which is the source of his power and vitality. His Nazirite rank and his ties to God came to remove the mythological elements in the story. There is a special relationship between God and Samson, thus, Samson is called נזיר אלהים *nazir Elohim* "consecrated one of God" (Judg 13:5,7;16:7).

Conclusion

Samson's Nazirite vow is mentioned only in the birth narrative and at the end of the story. If the reader did not read the story of his birth, he would not suspect that Samson was a Nazirite. Lifelong Nazirite ranking is unknown from the text of the Ancient Near East. The mention of Samson the Nazirite came to serve theological needs for the editors of the stories. In other words, Samson's heroic stature is a result of God's power. The connection between Samson and God is the Nazirite vow that God imposed on Samson's mother. The usage of the Nazirite vow and the motif of hair came to de-mythologize the image of Samson. Not as a mythical hero but as an Israelite hero who received his power from God. Reading the stories about

Samuel shows that there is no evidence that Samuel acted as a Nazirite. On the contrary, Samuel is acting as a priest, prophet, and a judge, never as a Nazirite. The origins of Nazirites are rooted in a holy war. The fighting man took a vow and let their hair grow during the time of war.

Samson's Nazirite status is found only in the birth narrative (13:5, 7) and at the end of the story (16:17). These verses have a religious flavor, while on the other hand, the description of his life and adventures in chapters 14–16 are secular in nature. This discrepancy led scholars to believe that chapter 13 originated at a later date than the following stories. Hence, in the following chapter we will examine the literary structure of the Samson story.

3

Literary Structure

SAMSON IS A UNIQUE character among the judges. He does not lead his people into war like the other judges. To the contrary, he is a single hero who fights empty-handed against his foes. He does not end oppression, and his battles are a result of his personal feuds with the Philistines. All of his feuds are outcomes of his involvement with Philistine women: the Taminite, the harlot from Gaza, and Delilah. The stories about Samson open with the announcement of his upcoming birth and end in his tragic death. Samson is a man of passion who loved women, but he never made a home in Israel. Hence, he is different from the other judges who were blessed with many children. Samson is the last judge in the Book of Judges. The stories about him are found in chapters 13–16 and are more than any other judge. There are three major parts to the story: The birth account 13:1–25; the parallel life accounts (14:1–15:20); and the death account (16:1–31).

Examination of these three blocks reveals a striking contrast between chapter 13, which has a religious flavor describing Samson's nativity account, and the description of his life and adventures in chapters 14–16, which are secular in nature. This discrepancy led scholars to believe that chapter 13 originated at a later date than the following stories. Modern scholars suggest that the ancient storyteller or the editor took popular folk hero legends and added a theological interpretation.[1] Indeed, source J is found in chapter 13 while there are no traces of it in chapters 14–16. Another break in the story is the source of Samson's powers. In chapters 14–15, Samson has his power as a result of "the spirit of Yahweh rushed upon him" (14:6, 9; 15:14). While in the story of the prostitute, he is naturally strong.

---

1. Kim, *Structure of the Samson Cycle*, xii

Similarly, the story of Samson and Delilah does not mention that "the spirit of Yahweh rushed upon him"; instead his strength is connected to his hair. Another clear break is at 15:20 where: "He judged Israel during the time of the Philistines for twenty years." This typical formula ending is repeated again in 16:31b: "he had judged Israel for twenty years." This suggests that the story of Samson and Delilah and the death of Samson were not an integral part of the original story. In other words, the verse in 15:20 was the first ending of the earlier Samson story, and to this first ending writers made additions later.

The existence of breakdowns in the story led Brettler to point out that: "Judges 13–16 have a complex history and derive from various sources which have been combined…The Samson cycle represents a model of redaction that is weak from a thematic and stylistic perspective." [2] Nevertheless, he points out that despite the different structure and different aspects of each unit, they actually do fit together. There are similarities between the units, thus he believes that elements were moved from one story to another, or they were transferred by an editor to create a more homogenous cycle.[3] This chapter will show that literary unity exists in the Samson story. There are internal themes that connect the Samson materials together. As Niditch points out: "The tales of Samson are characterized by recurring language motifs, and patterns of content."[4] We will demonstrate that religious flavor is not only found in chapter 13 but also exists in chapters 14–16. Additionally, the story is not only homogenous, but also connects to other stories in Judges, and 1Samuel.

The Birth of Samson

Scholars suggest that Judges 13:2–24 is an independent unit. It is an annunciation story that tells the miraculous birth of Samson and his status as a Nazirite.[5] In contrast, chapters 14–15 never recognize Samson as a Nazirite, the connection between his miraculous birth, his role as a Nazirite, and his great strength.[6] Hence, it was suggested that chapter 13, which introduces Samson's unbelievable birth, is only an introduction to Samson

---

2. Brettler, *Judges*, 58–60
3. Ibid., 58–9.
4. Niditch, *Judges*, 153.
5. Alter, "How Conventions Help Us Read," 115–30; Amit, *Judges*, 291–93.
6. Brettler, *Judges*, 43.

the man. It is not an introduction to the events that follow and the main themes that are narrated. Therefore, Judges 13:2–24 should be separated from the rest of the surrounding material.[7]

A through reading of the Samson cycle clearly indicates the opposite. The annunciation story is an integral part of the Samson story containing many motifs that appear in this story and are mentioned later in the cycle. More so the story is similar to other stories in the biblical narrative. As previously noted in chapter 1, the story of the birth of Samson is similar to Genesis 18, which describes the announcement of the birth of Isaac. In both stories are barren women: Sarah then Samson's mother. These stories describe the appearance of God or his angels during the daytime disguised as humans. In both of these stories a meal is served. In Genesis the meal is eaten, and in our story it is only offered.[8]

This story also shows affinities to Judges 6:11–24, which tells of the commission of Gideon to a judge. An angel of the Lord appeared to Gideon in human disguise during the daytime. In Judges 6 a meal is served which, was consumed by fire. In this story a meal is offered by Manoah to the angel. He offered to prepare a kid for the messenger, the same type of meal that Gideon offered the angel. In the Gideon story the meal was consumed by fire and in the Samson story the angel ascended in flames from the altar. In both stories, Gideon and Manoah expressed their fear of dying because they saw the angel of God. In the Gideon story, it is the angel who assured Gideon that he would not die, while in the Samson story it is Manoah's wife who tells her husband they would not die. Gideon was commissioned by the angel to save Israel from the hands of the Midianites, while Samson was commissioned to save Israel from the hands of the Philistines. These are not merely coincidental details. What the narrator tried to achieve here was to show continuity between previous stories in the Hebrew Bible and Samson's story. Not only is the story similar to another story in the Hebrew Bible, but it is also linked directly to the Book of Judges as the Gideon story testifies.

According to the message [that was delivered to Samson's mother by the angel], even before Samson was born he was to be a Nazirite: "no razor shall come upon his head, for the boy shall be a Nazirite to God from birth"

---

7. Ibid.

8. Some scholars compare our story to 1Sam1 where Hannah Samuel mother was barren and to the story of Rachel who was also barren. However, the matrix in our story is different. There is no prayer to God here instead a divine messengers comes in human form. See: Reinhartz, "Samson's Mother," 25–37; Ackerman, *Warrior Dancer, Seductress, Queen*, 181–207.

(13:5). This communication is repeated by Samson's mother to her husband Manoah (v.7). But more importantly, this motif of Samson the Nazirite appears again at the end of the story when Samson's hair is cut off by Delilah: "... a razor has never come upon my head; for I have been a Nazirite to God from my mother's womb. If I be shaved, then my strength will leave me ..." (16:17). Thus, the narrator created a link between the beginning of our story and the end of the story. What he tried to convey here is that Samson is a Nazirite from the womb, not for a specific period, but for life. Samson had a special relationship with God, which is manifested by his Nazirite status. The uncut hair symbolizes this special relationship between him and God. Indeed, as long as the symbol of his sacredness remains— which is his hair—the divine power that he received would be within him. This power left him after Delilah shaved his hair. The narrator stressed: "and had him shave off the seven locks of his head ... and his strength left him" (16:20c). The hair is mentioned again in the last scene before Samson's death where we read: "the hair of his head began to grow again after he was shaven" (v.22). Samson started to gain back his divine powers with the growth of his hair. This verse serves as a bridge to Samson's final act, which ended his life in a tragic fashion. With the growth of his hair, the symbol of his Nazirite status is retrieved. Hence, his mother's words rang true when she spoke about her son being a Nazirite: "until the day of his death" (13:7). As Amit pointed out, the hair of Samson's Nazirite status distinguished him, setting him apart, pointing to his special connection to God.[9] More so, we believe that the Naziritehood which is expressed by hair, serves as one of the components that links the Samson cycles together.

Samson, is from the tribe of Dan (13:1). He starts to operate at the borders of his tribe (v.25). When Samson is born: "The spirit of Yahweh began to stir him in the encampment of Dan between *Zorah and Eshtaol.*" The next time that the places *Zorah and Eshtaol* appear is when Samson dies; we read that his family buried him between *Zorah and Eshtaol* at the tomb of his father Manoah. By mentioning these places, the narrator further connects the opening of the story with the end of the story. More so, it says that he was buried in his father tomb. The identical site for Samson's election and burial is similar to the Gideon story. Accordingly, Gideon was elected at Ophrah of the Abi-ezrites, the place where he was later buried, which was also in the grave of his father Joash (Judg 8:31).

---

9. Amit, *Judges*, 278.

Literary Structure

Chapters 17–18 follow the Samson cycle and describe the establishment of Micah's shrine and the story of the Danites' migration. In chapter 18, in particular, we read about the Danites from *Zorah and Eshtaol* (18:2, 8, 11); hence, creating a link to the Samson story. They were looking for a new territory to settle in. The search for a new territory is the outcome of Samson's failure to deliver his people from the Philistines' yoke, therefore they moved to the north.

Delilah, whom Samson loved, betrayed him to the Philistines for the sum of 1,100 shekels of silver. As a result Samson lost his eyesight, strength, freedom (16:20–21), and ultimately, his life. In the Micah's story he confesses to his mother for the thievery of 1,100 silver pieces that he took from her, the same amount that Delilah received. In the Delilah story, money was exchanged between two consenting parties, while in the Micah story money was stolen. More so, Micah stole it from his own mother, thus he betrayed the blood tie of mother son kinship.[10] His betrayal surpasses Delilah's coaxing of Samson, since Micah was an Israelite who betrayed an Israelite. Moreover, he broke one of the Ten Commandments. At the end of the story, the Danites took the sculpture image, the ephod, the teraphim, and molten images from Micah's house. Those cultic objects were made from the money that was stolen by Micah, now it is the Danites who stole the cultic images. By mentioning the Danites in the Micah story, the author created continuity with the Samson cycle, informing the reader of what happened to the Danites following Samson's death. More so, it came to show the turmoil and chaos that existed in those days: "In those days there was no king in Israel" (17:6;18:1; 19:1;21:25), which is the crux of the action in the Book of Judges.

When Samson was born the spirit of God seized him. This motif of the spirit of Yahweh is repeated numerous times 14:6; 19; and 15:14. By mentioning the spirit of Yahweh, the narrator tells the reader that Samson's mighty acts were dependent on God who gave Samson the divine power. It connects the stories and gives them a religious flavor. On the other hand, there are some places were the spirit of the Lord is not mentioned such as when he went to the harlot in Gaza or when he stayed with Delilah. This is the start of Samson's decline, therefore the narrator did not mention the spirit of the Lord. The spirit of the Lord is not mentioned in places where doubt arises regarding the nature of the miraculous actions of Samson such as in the cases of scraping the honey, sending the foxes, or the killing of

---

10. Klein, *Triumph of Irony*, 143.

unknown numbers of Timnah's inhabitants.[11] Although the spirit is not mentioned in the last chapter of his life, after his hair was cut off, no one doubts the spirit acted within him there as well.

From birth, Samson's task was to save Israel from the hand of the Philistines: "He shall be the first to deliver Israel from the Philistines" (13:5). Examination of the following chapters reveals that all his life he fought against the Philistines and he saved Israel. Indeed, he appears as a savior in 15:18: "Thou hast given this great deliverance by the hand of Thy servant." His last words, "let me die with the Philistines" (16:30), also points to the fact that he started to deliver Israel. The fact that Samson started to deliver Israel is also conveyed by the formula: "And he Judged Israel in the days of the Philistines twenty years" (15:20). This editorial note is repeated again at the end of chapter 16: "He had judged Israel twenty years" (31c). This repetition has led scholars to believe that this editorial notation is marking the end of a large narrative segment and not leading to the final chapter. However, we should point out that repetition is the classical tool used by the biblical narrator to stress a point to deliver a message. What the author conveys here is that the victory at Lehi and the prayer for water signify the first part of Samson's life, which includes his victories against the Philistines. Therefore, the narrator used the formula, "he led Israel", while 16:20, which marked his tragic death, "he had led Israel," is in past perfect tense. (More details on this point in chapter 8.) Noteworthy is the language "he had led," which is found only with Eli in a note that appears after his death (1Sam 4:18).

A Broken Vow

Examination of the Samson story shows that chapter 13 serves as a bridge to the adventures of Samson in the subsequent chapters. At the center is a religious theme of a Nazirite vow. What is left for the reader to discover: Would Samson fulfill his Nazirite vow?[12] According to the vow, he must evade contact with a dead body, must not drink wine or other intoxicants, and most importantly, must not allow his hair to be cut during the period of his vow. It is believed that this form of vow originated during this period when the Israelites came into contact with the population of Canaan with

---

11. Amit, *Judges*, 279.
12. Blenkinsopp, "Structure and Style," 65–76.

their chthonic and orgiastic cults.[13] Only later was the vow changed to become a temporary vow. The vow was connected to a holy war and was considered an act of a young man or warrior, which in this case was Samson.

As noted already in our previous chapter, Samson broke all the Nazirite vows. In his second journey to Timnah, he encounters a lion that came roaring at him. The spirit of the Lord gripped him and he killed the lion. Returning the following year to marry the Philistine woman, he ate honey from the carcasses of the lion (v.9). By doing so he violated the first regulation.

Upon his marriage, Samson made a marriage feast as young men used to do. It is believed that heavy drinking was part of this celebration. If that was the case, Samson broke the second regulation here. On this occasion, Samson tells the participants a riddle. Later his wife will use guile to obtain the answer. The rest (14–15:1–8) reveals the consequences of the Philistines obtaining the answer to the riddle by being cunning. This will lead Samson to retaliate against the Philistines.

The last chapter in the Samson narrative is his alliance with Delilah, yet another Philistine woman. As with the woman from Timnah, Delilah also used guile in order to discover the secret of Samson's strength. After failing three times to obtain the secret of his strength, she finally succeeds. By revealing his secret, Samson broke the third part of his vow to not shave. Most tellingly is the fact that Samson broke each of his Nazirite vows in the order they were outlined in chapter 13. It's no surprise the shaving of hair appeared last. This order confirms our belief in a well thought-out plot.[14]

As noted previously, there is a striking contrast between chapter 13 describing Samson's nativity account, which has a religious flavor, with the description of his life and adventures in chapters 14–16, which are secular in nature. Despite Samson breaking all of his Nazirite vows, examination of chapters 14–16 shows that they are interspersed with religious elements. Samson's actions and deeds in chapters 14–16 are inspired by the Spirit of the Lord (14:6, 19; 15:14). In two places Samson is praying to God. At Enhakkore of Lehi, Samson is praying to God to save him from dying of thirst (15:18). At the temple of Dagon, he called on the Lord to give him strength to take revenge on the Philistines. In these two incidents God harkened to Samson's prayers. Samson's final victory over the Philistines at the temple of their god Dagon, with God's assistance, proves above all the religious nature of the whole cycle. The Samson story is a masterful piece of work

13. Ibid., 65.
14. Ibid., 66.

written by a skillful writer. The story is homogenous and describes the life of Samson. It is a literary biography of our hero. It appears in a logical order, a well thought-out plot, which starts with the announcement of the birth of Samson and ends with his death. Any attempt to remove or change some parts of the story will damage the harmony, unity, and logical structure of the story.

Chapters 14–15

It is suggested that chapters 14–15 are a coherent unit, which distinguishes them from preceding events and that which follows them. These chapters contain four episodes. The first episode (14:1–20) describes Samson's desire to marry a Philistine woman at Timnah; the slaying of a lion; the riddle and its interpretation at the wedding feast; and the revenge slaughter of 30 Philistines from Ashkelon. The second episode (15:1–8) recounts how Samson's father-in-law rejects Samson's attempt to get close to his wife. As a result of this, Samson burned the Philistine's fields. This led to the burning of his wife and father-in-law by the Philistines. Samson retaliates by defeating the Philistines, and he retreats to the cave in Eitam. In the third episode, Samson is bound by the men of Judah who delivered him to the Philistines (15:9–13). In the fourth and final episode (15:14–19), Samson kills 3,000 Philistines. In addition, we read of his thirst and prayers to God, which resulted in the creation of a spring by God.

Brettler tries to tie these chapters to the wisdom literature and claims that wisdom tradition is behind chapters 14–15.[15] But examination of these stories shows the evidence is weak supporting his theory.[16] Chapter 14–15 are not only a coherent unit but are also connected to chapter 16. Samson's intentions and desire to marry a Philistine woman at Timnah are mentioned in 14:2. This opening statement is key to understanding Samson's involvement with Philistine women, which is narrated in chapters 14–16. The author says: "His father and mother did not realize that this was the Lord's doing: He was seeking a pretext against the Philistines" (14:4). In other words, Samson's desire does not stem from lust, but it was from God. It is God who stirs Samson, he is a tool in God's hands. God is behind the scenes and Samson is acting. Block summarizes God's action: "Yahweh is determined to shatter the status quo. Samson is his tool chosen to rile up

---

15. Brettler, *Judges*, 50–51
16. Butler, *Judges*, 333.

LITERARY STRUCTURE

the Philistines, and this woman offers the opportunity to make it happen."[17] This verse gives the reader insight into God's plan, therefore, the reader knows more than Samson's parents.

Samson's involvement with a Philistine woman is not limited to chapter 14 but also appears in 15–16. Women played a major role in his life. It is this involvement that sets our stories into motion, connecting them to each other. It was suggested that the goal of presenting women in the Samson cycle was to denounce Samson as a Judge who did not have any national interest.[18] Indeed, in the Hebrew Bible we have instances where women are described as the reason for the hero's failure. We find in this category David and Bathsheba, as well as Solomon and his wives who turned him to worship other gods, then again with Ahab who married Jezebel who served and worshiped Baal.

According to Zakovitch, the mention of the parents at the start of the chapter (14:1–4) is a later motif and is not part of the original narrative.[19] Accordingly, the chapter should start with v.5.[20] However, the parents link our chapter to a previous chapter (13). More so, we have to remember that parents initiated marriages in ancient times, so without them the marriage could not take place. Verses 5–11 describe the events that preceded the wedding feast. Samson went down to Timnah and he killed a lion (14:56); later he ate honey from the lion's skeleton (vv.8–9). These two events play a major role in the wedding feast where Samson presents a riddle to the guests.

Celebrating his marriage, Samson entertains the guests with a riddle and challenges them to solve it within the seven days of the wedding celebrations. Since there was no way for the Philistines to know the answer, they asked Samson's wife to cajole him into divulging the answer to the riddle. Once they knew the secret answer to the riddle, Samson had to pay his debt with clothing for 30 Philistines. He does this by killing 30 people at Ashkelon. Killing 30 Philistines does not seem dramatic enough in light of the angel's prediction. Thus, the reader is left with an open question: How will Samson fulfill his divine task against the Philistines?[21]

---

17. Block, *Judges, Ruth*, 426.
18. Amit, *Judges*, 280.
19. Zakovitch, *Life of Samson*, 88–100.
20. Simpson suggested that the story started with v. 5 without *and his father and his mother* and *to Timnah*. See: Simpson, *Composition of the Book of Judges*, 57
21. Broida, "Closure in Samson," 18.

The Samson Story

Returning to visit his wife, Samson discovered that she was given to his best man. This led Samson to take revenge against the Philistines. He tied the tails of 150 foxes, placing a torch between each pair of tails, setting them on fire, then sent them into the Philistine's fields. The Philistine's fields were burned down, which led to the back and forth retaliation between Samson and the Philistines. Since Samson set their fields on fire, the Philistines took Samson's wife and her father and put them into the fire. In other words, what we have here is measure for measure. Burning was a severe punishment that was reserved in Israel for adultery.[22] Samson's wife committed adultery when she was given to another man by her father. She is killed by fire because of Samson's actions, and as noted, death by fire, ironically, was reserved for adultery. In retaliation for the death of his wife and her father, Samson kills many more Philistines.

There is an attempt by the Philistines to trap Samson (9–17). They turn to the people of Judah and asked them to deliver Samson into their hands. The Philistine's objective was vengeance against Samson (15:10b), hence, it connects them to the Philistines in the previous episode. The people of Judah, according to the text: ". . . bound him with two new ropes." (15:13). When Samson was delivered to the Philistines: "and the ropes on his arms became like flax which caught fire; the bonds melted off his hands" (v.14). The way that Samson was tied and his reaction to the Philistine's act foreshadows the next story of Samson with Delilah where these elements are repeated. Delilah tied Samson three times. The first time was with the fresh bow strings, which had not been dried (16: 6–9); the second time was with the new ropes that had not been used (10–12); and a third time was with the web made tight with the pin. The way that Samson released himself is similar to the previous episode (15:14), hence, three times we find how he released himself: "Whereat he pulled the tendons apart, as a strand of tow comes apart at the touch of fire" (16:9); "But he tore them off his arms like a thread"(v.12); "he pulled out the peg, the loom and the web"(v.14).

In addition, the simile in 15:14, "the ropes melted off his arms like flax burned with fire" not only foreshadows the story of Samson and Delilah, but this links the scene to the fire in unit two (15:5–6). In other words, it creates cohesion to the entire story.[23]

The story of Samson's thirst is the continuation of his great victory at Lehi (15:18–19). It is not an independent story, and indeed, Samson

---

22. For the subject of the death by burning see: Bar, "Punishment of Burning," 27–39.
23. Broida, "Closure in Samson," 20.

LITERARY STRUCTURE

mentions here the great victory that God granted him. Like the previous story, this etiological story explains the origin of the place and the meaning of its name. The reason for his thirst, according to the Midrash, was the result of what he said in an unnecessary and arrogant manner.[24] More so, the Midrash says: "Even had there been a goblet of water before him, he could not have stretched out his hand to take it" being so exhausted.[25] God saves Samson from a desperate situation. This is the only time in the Samson cycle that Samson is not using his strength; he remains passive. His call to God was repeated before his last heroic deed (16:28). The recurring calls by Samson to God underscore that in spite of God's spirit coming upon him, the hero is aware of his dependence on God as the source of his strength.[26] The aim of this story is to diminish Samson's image as a mighty hero who is unstoppable and can overcome every obstacle. Instead, the narrator inserts a religious flavor to our story by stating it was not Samson's own power behind his victory, but it was God's blessings. Furthermore, Samson's prayer to God shows us how much he depends on God. This was noted by Josephus who says:

> Yet Samson, unduly proud of this feat, did not say that it was God assistance that had brought it to pass, but ascribed the issue to his own valor, boasting of having with a jawbone prostrated some of the enemies and put the rest to rout through the terror that he inspired. But, being seized with a mighty thirst and recognizing that the human valor is a thing of naught, he acknowledged that all was attributable to God and implored Him not, in anger at any words of his, to deliver him into his enemies hands, but to lend him aid in his dire need and to rescue him from his distress. And God, moved by his applications, caused a spring of water to well out of a rock, sweet and abundant; whence it was that Samson called that place Jawbone, a name which it bears to this day.[27]

God heeds to Samson's plea for water and splits open the hollow, and as a result, water comes out of it. This type of description, where God brings out water for the thirsty one, is a recurring motif (Num 20:8; Isa 48:21; Ps 78:15–16; 105:41; Neh 9:15). The most notable example is when Moses struck the rock in order to get water. The narrator probably

---

24. *Gen. R.* 98:13
25. Ibid.
26. Amit, *Judges*, 279.
27. Josephus, *Antiquities*. 5.9.

was familiar with this story and borrowed it in order to show Samson's dependence on God.

The Downfall

The third segment of Samson's stories contains three episodes that lead to his death. In the first, Samson visits a prostitute and carries the gates of Gaza (16:1–3). The second one is the story of Samson and Delilah (16:4–22). The last episode narrates the events at the Dagon temple and Samson's death (16:23–31). The story of Samson and the harlot from Gaza opens the last part of the Samson stories. At first glance, it appears to be an independent story that is not connected to the events that precede it and the stories that follow it. However, a close reading of the story reveals otherwise. The story is narrated in three verses (16:1–3). Samson goes to Gaza where he stays at the house of a harlot. The harlot's name remains anonymous, just as with the previous women with whom Samson engages. The fact that Samson slept with the harlot was the beginning of his downfall. In other words, Samson began to sin in Gaza, and therefore, he was punished in Gaza. As we pointed out previously, Samson sinned with his eyes: "Once Samson went down to Timnah; and while in Timnah *he saw* a girl among the Philistines" (14:1). Similarly, in our episode, when Samson came to Gaza we are told he: "*saw there a harlot*" and he was attracted to her (16:1). Therefore, later his eyes were extracted.[28]

Josephus notes the connection between this story and the previous episode that took place at Lehi. According to him after the battle in Lehi, Samson was not afraid of the Philistines when he enters their city: "After this combat [lehi] Samson, scorning the Philistines, came to Gaza and lodged at one of the inns."[29] A connection to the previous chapter also appears in the Alexandrian version of the LXX where: "And Samson went from there to Gaza." Amit rejected this connection and pointed to the formula: "He led Israel in the days of the Philistines for twenty years" (Judg 15:20). However, according to Moore, the words "from there" were original and dropped from the Masoretic text because of the inclusion of the judging formula.[30] Hence, he suggested that there was a moment in time where chapter 16 was the direct continuation of chapter 15.

28. b. Soṭah. 9b.
29. Josephus, *Atniquities*.5.10.
30. Moore, *Judges*, 350.

Literary Structure

Not only is there a connection to the previous chapters, but our story resonates with the story of Rahab and the spies in Joshua.[31] In both of these stories, Israelites went to the house of a harlot. The townspeople tried to capture them but they failed. The women are referred to as harlots (Josh 2:1; 6:22; Judg 16:1). In the Samson story: "there he met a whore," while in the Rahab story "they came to the house of a harlot." In the two stories, the townspeople were informed that their enemies were in their town (Judg 16:2; Josh 2:2). This rumor is described in a similar language: "Samson had come there" (Judg 16:2); "Some man have come here)" (Josh 2:2). Samson "lay in bed only until midnight" (16:3); the spies "lodged there" (Josh 2:1). Gates are mentioned in both stories. Samson put the gates on his shoulders and carried them (Judg 16:3). In the Rahab story "when the gate was about to be closed," (Josh 2:5); "the gate was shut behind them" (v.7). Samson left the city in an unusual way, as did the spies who went down from the window by rope (2:15). Samson carried the gates of Gaza to the mountain (Judg. 16:3), while the spies escaped to the mountain (Josh 2:16, 22, 23). As Zakovitch pointed out, the similarity between the stories also shows the differences between them. In the story about Samson and the harlot, Samson is the main character: he arrives, he sleeps, then carries the gates. The harlot, on the other hand, has no role; she is passive. Quite the opposite happens in the Rahab story where she plays a major role. She hides the spies and helps them to escape before deceiving the messengers from the King of Jericho.[32]

The story of Samson and the Gazite harlot is also connected chronologically to the story that follows, which is Samson and Delilah "After that" (v.4). Samson plucked the gate of Gaza humiliating the philistines. As a result, the Philistines are ready to pay a high price to Delilah for her to surrender Samson into their hands. When the Philistines incarcerate Samson they bring him to Gaza, the city he took the gates from. The last heroic deed that was performed by Samson was the destruction of the temple of Dagon, which also took place in Gaza. In other words, all the events take place in Gaza.

There is also a clear connection in the language. The root ʾrb (to lie in wait); "and *lay in wait* for him" (v.2) appears later in the story about Delilah "now she had men *lying in wait*" (vv. 9, 12). The verb nsʾ ("to pull up") and "*pulled them up*" (v.3); "and *pulled away* the pin ... " (v.14). Samson is carrying the gates, while at the end of the chapter Samson prays to God to

---

31. Zakovitch, *Life of Samson*, 162–63.
32. Ibid., 163.

help him to bring down the pillars (v.3, 21).³³ Crenshaw points to the similarities between the name "Delilah" and the word for night לילה (*layelah*), which is found four times in the story about the gates of Gaza.³⁴ This may partly explain the juxtaposition of these two stories. But his interpretation for the name Delilah is unlikely because the name is probably a short theophoric name that appears in Akkadian names such as Dalil Ishtar or Dilil Ishtar, which refers to the Glory of Ishtar.

The story of Samson and Delilah is not only connected to the Gazite harlot but also to the story of Samson and his wife (chapter 14). At the center of these two stories is the element of enticement. In both stories, a woman entices Samson to reveal his secrets. In the first story, it's the secret of the riddle, and in the second it's the secret of his strength. To underscore this resemblance, the narrator uses the same word "entice." In both stories, we find a similar dialogue. Delilah accuses Samson: "How can you love me when your heart is not with me?" (16:15). This accusation echoes Samson's wife's words: "You only hate me, you don't love me!" (14:16). In both stories the women harass Samson, and the narrator again uses the same vocabulary הציקתהו *hṣîqthû* in 14:17; הציקה לו *hṣîqh lô* and in 16:16. This harassment took place for a while, in the first story for seven days and in the second story it was all the days. To stress the irritation and aggravation of the harassment, the narrator added the words: "shortening his life until his death." Finally, when Samson tells Delilah his secret, he tells her: "No razor shall go over my head, for I am a Nazirite to God from my mother's womb" (16:17a), hence mentioning the specific instruction given by the angel to his parents in Chapter 13. The Delilah story ends with the shaving of Samson's hair, the same hair that was not supposed to be shaved. As a result, not only did Samson's strength depart from him, but the Lord departed from him as well. To give the reader some glimpse of hope and to lead to the last episode, the narrator tells us that Samson's hair started to grow. The author of our story created continuity using the motif of Samson's hair and his Nazirite status, which is found in the first block of our narrative connecting to the last part of the Samson story; hence by doing so he added coherence to the narrative.

The final episode (16:23–31) starts with jubilation and celebration. The Philistines are gathering to thank their god Dagon for their triumph over Samson. In their joy they proclaim: "Our God gave our enemy into our

---

33. Amit, *Judges*, 283.
34. Crenshaw, *Samson*, 18–19.

hand" (v.23). These words resonate with Samson, fearful of falling into the hands of the Philistines (15:18). In the next scene the Philistines bring Samson to entertain them. The biblical narrator describes the temple, which is jam-packed with all the Philistine lords and 3,000 men and women. In contrast to his heroic stature, Samson now appears helpless when he is asking God for guidance to go between the pillars on which the temple stands. As the reader recalls, Samson already prayed to God to save his life from the hands of the Philistines (15:18). Here, in contrast, Samson prays for death: "Let me die with the Philistines." In both instances God answered his prayer. It is noteworthy that the words "Let me die with the Philistines" closely mirror and predict Samson's words to Delilah "he was wearied to death" (16:16).

Samson and the Book of Samuel

The story of Samson's birth shares some similarities with the birth of Samuel. The opening statement in the Samson story: "And there was a certain man of Zorah . . . " (Judg 13:2), and the Samuel story: "And there was certain man of Ramathaim Zophim (1Sam 1:1). These are the only cases in which this formula is found in the Hebrew Bible. It is believe that both Samson and Samuel are lifelong Nazirites, in contrast to the biblical law that limits the time of Nazirite status. Their birth narrative is similar. The names of their parents are given, a barren mother who prays for a child. A child is promised and he would be a Nazirite. In the Samuel story it was Hannah who took a vow that her future son would be a lifelong Nazirite. While in the Samson story, this was ordered by the angel of the Lord. Still the restrictions are identical in both stories. There is a cultic atmosphere in the stories, which concludes with everlasting dedication made under the influence of the רוח *ruaḥ YAHWH*.[35] Samuel like Samson fights against the Philistines (1Sam 7), but the story is generalized. Hence, it was suggested that it is a production of a later prophetic revision. In other words, Samuel is not a warrior like Samson.[36]

In the Hebrew canon, the Book of Samuel appears after the Book of Judges. Not surprisingly, Samson did not deliver the Israelites from the hands of the Philistines, so the continued fighting against the Philistines is described in detail in the Book of Samuel. More so, there is a recurring theme. Samson

---

35. Blenkinsopp, "Structure and Style," 70
36. Brooks, "Saul and the Samson Narrative," 21.

The Samson Story

killed a lion singlehandedly, similarly, we read about David who boasted to King Saul: "Your servant has killed both lion and bear ... " (1Sam 17:36). Samson went to Ashkelon and killed 30 of its men; Jonathan and his armsbearer killed some 20 men at Geba (1Sam14:14); while David fought against Goliath and killed him. These heroic actions describing the Israelites fighting against the Philistines were evidently very popular stories that remained in the memories of the Israelites because of their special nature.

As we mentioned, the Philistines turned to the people of Judah asking them to deliver Samson into their hands because they failed to capture him. The people of Judah complied and delivered Samson. Later, a similar story during the reign of King Saul is recorded. Accordingly, there were two different groups of people who wanted to capture David and deliver him to Saul. The first were the inhabitants of Keilah, which David saved from the Philistines. They were ungrateful people who were afraid of David's presence in their city. Therefore, they were willing to betray David. The second was the Ziphites, who took the initiative informing Saul of David's hiding place. They probably heard of the slaughter of the priests of Nob, as well as the destruction of the city that included its inhabitants. Although they were members of David's tribe of Judah, they wanted to show their loyalty to the king, therefore they divulged David's hiding place.

Many similarities are also found between Saul and Samson. Both appear as a result of the Philistine's oppression. Their role was to liberate the Israelites from that oppression. About Samson we read: "and he shall begin to liberate Israel from the Philistines power," (13:5), and about Saul it is written: "and he shall liberate my people from the Philistines power" (1Sam. 9:15). Saul and Samson received the divine spirit to free their people by performing heroic actions. In the Samson story, we read: "And the spirit of the Lord gripped him, and he tore him asunder ... ," (Judg 14:6, 19). In the Saul story: "And the spirit of God rushed upon Saul in power ... he took a yoke of oxen, and cut them into pieces ... " (1Sam 11:6–7). Samson tore a lion, while Saul tore a yoke of oxen, and in both instances they feel the surge of strength. In Judges 14:19 Samson became enraged, and similarly, Saul became enraged (1Sam 11:6).[37] The spirit of Yahweh left Samson after Delilah shaved him. In the Saul story: "Now the spirit of Yahweh departed from Saul ... " (1Sam 16:14). Saul disobeyed Samuel twice, he did not follow his instructions. He offered sacrifice despite Samuel's orders not to do so. He did it because he felt hard-pressed; the Philistines had gathered at Michmas

---

37. Ibid., 21.

Literary Structure

and his people were leaving him and scattering (13: 11). The second time he violated the ban, he did not destroy Amalek. In this instance, he yielded to pressure from his troops (15:9, 15). Similarly, Samson was also weakened under pressure. This pressure was of a different kind, it was put on him by his Philistine wife (Judg 14:16–18) and by Delilah (16:16–17). As a result, Samson revealed the secret of his strength, which led to his downfall. In other words, Samson and Saul broke under pressure, which led them both to their demise. Both men died in their last battle against the Philistines. Saul died in Mount Gilboa and Samson at the temple of Dagon. Their tragic death was suicidal in both scenarios. Samson for his last act: "Samson cried, "Let me die with the Philistines!" and he pulled with all his might. The temple came crashing down on the lords and on all the people in it ..." (Judg 16:30). While, King Saul is described as he: " ... grasped the sword and fell upon it."(1Sam 31:4).[38]

Conclusion

In conclusion, the Samson story is a masterful piece of work written by a skillful writer. The story is homogenous and describes the life of Samson from his birth to his death. It appears in a logical order and the stories are connected to each other. In addition, some of the stories are linked to previous stories in the Hebrew Bible and are based on them. The stories also show affinities to the Book of Samuel, which continues to describe the battles against the Philistines. Any attempt to remove or change some parts of the story would damage the continuity, harmony, unity, and logical structure of the story.

Women played a major role in Samson's life, thus in the next chapter we will analyze the three women who appear in the Samson cycle. We will compare these women and indicate the differences between them.

---

38. Brooks suggests that the parallels between Samson and Saul stem from the fact that: "the pro-Saul author could not openly write the true story of Saul; instead he camouflaged it behind the heroic image of Samson." See: Brooks, "Saul and Samson Narrative," 25.

4

Women in the Samson Story

IN THE HEBREW BIBLE, women appear, for the most part, as minor or subordinate figures. Not so in the Samson stories, where women play an important role in Samson's life. Not surprisingly, following the birth narrative of Samson, the first episode starts with him going down to Timnah where he sees a young Philistine woman. The second woman mentioned in the Samson stories is the harlot from Gaza and the third one is Delilah. When speaking about Samson and the women that he is involved with, the biblical narrator uses the verb to *see* (Judg 14:1; 16:1). It was only with Delilah that the narrator uses the verb to *love* (16:4). It is Samson who loves Delilah, however, Delilah was greedy, preferring 1,100 shekels of silver over his love. The deception motif plays a major role in these narratives. The stories in which devious women outsmart the man are a popular motif. This is found in the biblical narrative in stories about Yael (Judg 4–5), Esther, and Judith.[1] In those stories, the victorious women are Israelites. Not so in our story, where the foreign women have the upper hand; they are on the victorious side. Samson is entrapped by foreign women who betray him by revealing his secrets. The three foreign women who appear in the Samson story are bad; they are the subject of Samson's sexual desire. While the Bible usually speaks of a man seducing a woman in our stories there is role reversal; it is the Philistine women who overcome Samson by seduction.[2] To die at the hand of a woman was considered a disgrace; Deborah told Barak to go alone to war so it would not be said that the Lord delivered Sisera into the hands of a woman (4:9). Abimelech died after a woman dropped a millstone on

1. Crenshaw, *Samson*, 43–4.
2. Greenstein, "Riddle of Samson," 244.

his head. Samson, on the other hand, was defeated not by physical strength but by the powers of seduction, which makes this story a greater tragedy. In this chapter we will examine the characters of the Timnite the harlot, and Delilah to compare the differences between these three women.

The Timnite Woman

The story is divided into three sections:

1. Taking the Philistine as a wife (14:1–9).
2. The marriage banquet (14:10–19).
3. The marriage breakup(14:20; 15:1–7)

Each part begins with Samson going down to Timnah, and each time there is progress in the story. The relationship between Samson and the Philistine woman develops in stages. At first he sees her (Judg14:1), the second time he speaks to her (14:7), and the third time he marries her. In each of the three phases of the story, an event takes place that has significance for the development of the story.

Samson went down to Timnah, which is located six miles straight west of Zorah. It is identified with the ruined site of Tibneh, near the modern village of the same name. Timnah was originally allocated to the tribe of Dan (Josh 19:43). However, according to 15:10, it was located on Judah's northern border. At that time, the place was under the Philistine control. However, Samson could move freely between the Israelite territory and the Philistine's region. Evidently, during this period there were no direct conflicts between the Israelites and the Philistines.

In the ancient world, parents initiated marriages and chose a wife for their son. Hagar took a wife for her son Ishmael from Egypt. Abraham sent his servant with guidelines and instructions to pick a wife from his father's house for Isaac. Similarly, Isaac ordered Jacob to marry a wife from his family. Shechem, after he raped Dinah, told his father: "Get me this girl as a wife" (Gen 34:4). Likewise, Samson tells his parents: "I noticed one of the women in Timnah; please get her for me as a wife" (Judg14:2). Conversely, Esau picked his own wives who were Hittites. Since Isaac and Rebecca were grieved by his marriage, he went and married Mahalath, his cousin, the daughter of Ishmael. In ancient times, it was customary to marry within one's own clan, tribe, or family. The practice of endogamy, which is a marriage within the family, was customary in ancient times. This practice was a result of unfriendly relations with neighboring tribes or due to separation from a majority group.

The fact that Samson chose a foreign woman, especially a Philistine, was painful to his parents. They expressed their dissatisfaction by asking him if there were no acceptable women among his people and relatives. We have to remember that according to Deuteronomy 7:1–5, intermarriages were forbidden by the Lord. Samson's parents pointed out that the Philistines were uncircumcised. This was an important matter because according to Genesis 17:9–14, circumcision is a precondition for admittance into the community of Israelites, and Exodus 12:43–9 forbids an uncircumcised male to participate in the Passover sacrifice.

In spite of his parent's objections, Samson still asked his parents to get him the Philistine woman. Strangely, the woman is nameless and she does not even receive a title of honor such as "maiden" or "a maiden virgin." This led to suggest that she was a woman of questionable morals.[3] To express his desire for the Philistine woman he said: "she is right in my eyes." The motif of seeing by the eyes is repeated in our story: "The mention of eyes in the early stages of the plot is a hint and foreshadows the future when Samson loses his eyes. This was pointed out by the Rabbis: "Our Rabbis taught: Samson rebelled [against God] through his eyes, as it said, *And Samson said unto his father, Get her for me, because she is pleasing in my eyes*; therefore the Philistines put out his eyes."[4] More so, in Judges 17:6 and 21:25, we read "Each man does what is right in his own eyes," which describes the Israelites turning astray from the covenant. While with Samson we read "right in the eye," which evidently points out that something bad will happen. In other words, it refers to Samson following an alien culture and religion.

It appears as though Samson ignores his parents and shows disrespect toward them. But the narrator of our story inserted an editorial note: "His father and his mother did not know that this was from Yahweh, for he was seeking an occasion against the Philistines" (14:4). In other words, God is at work. This note also serves a theological explanation of Samson's future adventures. Although the parents did not know that this was from God, they stopped their objections to his request and went with Samson to Timnah. We are not told what caused them to change their mind. Therefore, it is possible that he convinced them to arrange his marriage.

---

3. Hertzberg, *Die Bücher Josua, Richter, Ruth*, 229.
4. *b. Soṭah. 9b.20*.

The story continues with Samson and his parents who went down to Timnah. It is believed that the words in verse 5 "his father and mother" were added later to the verse. This is because the second part of the verse describes Samson's encounter with a young lion. His parents are not mentioned there at all. More so, later in verse 10 we read "Now his father went concerning the woman." Thus, it is possible that Samson separated himself from his parents, for what happened next occurred without witness. According to Kaufamn, Samson knew the different back roads, while his parents used the high roads; hence Samson went between the vineyards.[5]

To describe his journey to Timnah, the biblical narrator says that Samson went down ירד (*yered*) and in contrast we find the verb עלה '*lah*—went up. As mentioned earlier, almost every action by Samson starts with him going down and then going up. Noteworthy is the similar vocabulary used to tie the stories of the Timnite woman and the harlot. Hence, Judges 14 starts: "Samson went down to Timnah and he saw a woman in Timnah." While Judges 16 starts: "Samson went to Gaza and he saw there a harlot." On the other hand, the sages compared this story to the story of Tamar Judah's daughter in law:

> "How is it that one verse says, *And Samson went down to Timnah* (14:1) and another verse says, *Behold thy father-in-law goes up to Timnah*? (Gen 38:13). Rab answered: There were two Timnahs; Judah's was one, and Samson's was another. R. Aibu, son of Nagare, explained that it was rather like the case of Beth Maon, which one reaches by *going down* from Pelugtah, and by going up from Tiberias. R. Simon agrees that there was only one Timnah, and the reason why the text speaks both of "going down" and "going up" is as follows: In Judah's case, where his acts were due to a high motive, it is described as "going up," while in the case of Samson where it was not due to any high motive, it is described as "going down." It is written, And they came to the vineyards of Timnah (Judg 14:5).[6]

The similarity between the two stories is not limited to the women's habitat. In the two stories a kid is given (Gen 38:17, 20; Judg 15:1). More so, a threat of setting the women on fire is mentioned in both stories (Gen 38:24; Judg 14:15).

The parents who played a major role in Samson's birth narrative are marginalized here. They went with him in order to arrange his marriage,

---

5. Kaufman, *Judges*, 251.
6. *Num. R.* 9:24.

but they are not mentioned at all in the story. It is possible that by removing them from the negotiations, the narrator wanted to stress their displeasure with Samson's choice. Samson speaks directly with the Tamnite, which is strange, since in the Patriarchal society the custom was to speak with the father or brother of the bride to be. We are told again that she was right in his eyes. Although, his parents are not mentioned, it is possible that they were present while he was speaking. It is noteworthy that there is no mention of the woman's parents either. This is in contrast to other biblical stories that dealt with marriages. Hence, when Abraham's servant went to bring a wife to Isaac, the Bible describes in detail how the servant negotiated with Rebecca's family. Similarly, we read how Hamor and Shechem negotiated with Jacob and his sons regarding the marriage proposal for Dinah. We are not told what the nature of the conversation was between Samson and the Philistine woman. More so, through the whole story, she remains nameless, she is simply referred to as Samson's wife. Malbim (1809–1879 acronym for Meir Loeb ben Yehiel Michael), suggested that Samson had a conversation with her to find out whether she was intelligent, because until now he had only seen her, therefore, we read in verse 6 *"she pleased Samson well."*

After some time passed, Samson went again to Timnah to claim his wife and to marry her. In other words, his previous visit was the engagement. It was a declaration of his will to marry her. He returns now to take her as his wife. This was consummated with the payment of the bridal price to her parents.

Samson's father went down to Timnah with Samson to participate in the marriage feast. Indeed, the second part of verse 10 tells that Samson made a feast there. This refers to the seven days of drinking at the home of the bride's parents. This custom is mentioned in the Patriarchal period (Gen 29:27) in Mesopotamia. It is practiced even in the twenty-first century because it is a rabbinical enactment.[7] The Hebrew word משתה *mišteh*, which describes the feast, connotes heavy drinking. Therefore, it appears that Samson broke his Nazirite vow as we noted in chapter 2. According to the Nazirite law (Num 6:2), he was supposed to separate himself from wine and strong drink; the mother of Samson was also ordered to abstain from any produce of the vine, even non-alcoholic (Judg 13:14). Still, we should point out that it is not written anywhere in the Bible that he was involved in drinking. Since he arranged the feast of drinking, it is assumed that he took part of it.

7. Ketub.7.

Women in the Samson Story

There is no description of the relationship between Samson and the intended woman. As mentioned above, Samson spoke to her and she was pleasing in his eyes. Now he came to take her and arranged a feast. What took place between them is not recorded. It is noteworthy that it was Samson who organized the feast. This is a glaring contrast to Laban the father of Rachel who gathered all the people of his place and made a feast upon his daughter's marriage to Jacob (Gen 29:22).

According to Crenshaw, the wedding between Samson and the woman may have been what he called a *tsadiqah*. He suggests that the rift between Samson and his parents was so great that Manoah arranged a special kind of marriage. In this arrangement, the wife remains in her father's home while the husband lives there with his wife, or he makes occasional visits.[8] This kind of marriage assured a woman protection by her household. In addition, it was also an advantage to herdsman who followed their cattle in search of pasture.

At the wedding, Samson was given 30 companions since the groom could not be alone. However, it is not clear why there were no Israelites among his companions; only Philistines are mentioned. The role of these companions is also not clear. The LXX translate this 'because they feared' him instead of 'when they saw him' (v.11). In other words, since they were afraid of him, they attached to him 30 bodyguards to protect themselves from him. Josephus, who was probably familiar with this version, says:

> Now the Thamnites, on the occasion of the wedding feast—for he entertained them all— from the fear of this young man's strength, presented him with thirty of their chief stalwarts, ostensibly as companions, in reality as his guardians, lest he should be minded to create any disturbances.[9]

Alternatively, the usage of the word מרעים *meraim* might point to the fact that these groups of Philistines were also friends of the groom and not only bodyguards. It is noteworthy that the noun מרע *meraʿ* appears four times in the narrative in reference to the Philistine (14:11, 20; 15: 2, 6). More so, the noun appears also in the Book of Genesis when it speaks of one of the friends of Abimelech the Philistine king of Gerar (Gen 26:26). This path was taken by Targum Jonathan that renders here חברין *ḥevarin* an expression of companions.

---

8. Crenshaw, *Samson*, 82.
9. Josephus, *Ant.* 5.289

Pressuring Samson's Wife

During the festivities celebrating his marriage, Samson entertains the Philistines with a riddle and challenges them to solve it within the seven days of the wedding celebrations. As Samson predicted, three days passed and the companions could not solve the riddle. Therefore, on the seventh day the Philistines went to Samson's wife and asked her to persuade her husband to provide them with the answer. If she refused, they would set her and her father's house on fire. They blamed her for putting them in such a precarious situation where they were going to lose their possessions. It is not their fault that they accepted Samson's challenge to solve the riddle, but now it is her fault because she invited them to her marriage feast.

Burning people to death was a bad omen that meant total obliteration of the dead. Execution by burning meant non-burial; this was the end to continuity and the final extinction of the deceased, who had not been "gathered to his ancestors."[10] Biblical law specifies burning as the punishment for two forms of illicit sex (Lev 20:14; 21:9). In the story of Achan, set at the time of the conquest of Canaan, burning is the punishment for sacrilege. In our story, burning is not a punishment imposed by a court of law. When people took the law into their hands, they used the threat of burning. In our case, the Philistine carried out the threat and they burned Samson's wife and her father in his house. It is noteworthy that the threat of burning appears also in the Book of Judges with the Jephthah story. The Ephramites, in their fury, threatened Jephthah that they would burn his house with him in it (Judg 12:1). According to v.1, the reason for their anger was because Jephthah did not call them to join him in his fight against the Ammonites.

Samson's wife tried to use her feminine charms to avoid the horrible punishment from her own people. She does as she was instructed by the Philistine "Coax your husband." Later, the Philistines will use the same language, asking Delilah to coax Samson to find out what makes him so strong. However, in Delilah's case, they did not use a threat. Instead, they bribed her. Trying to get the answer to the riddle, Samson's wife harassed him with tears and also with words: "You really hate me, you don't love me. You asked my countrymen a riddle, and you didn't tell me the answer" (Judg 14:16). This is the first time in the narrative that she speaks. She tries to blackmail Samson by accusing him that since he did not share his secrets with her, he does not love her. Later, Delilah uses similar words to find

---

10. See: Bar, "Punishment of Burning," 27–39.

the secret of Samson's strength, "How can you say you love me, when you don't confide in me? (16:15). In reply to her accusation, Samson said to his wife: "I haven't even told my father and mother; shall I tell you?"(14:16). The implication is that Samson had a more intimate and affectionate relationship with his parents than his wife. Samson's reply did not stop her from continuing to harass him with her tears during the seven days of the feast. This is a bit surprising because according to verses 15–16, she began her tearful pleas on the seventh day. Rashi solved it by interpreting it as the remainder of the seven days, from the fourth and onward. As for her continued harassment it was Ralbag who suggested that she tormented him by various means such as evading nuptial relations.

The turning point takes place on the seventh day. After constant nagging by his wife, Samson reveals to her the answer to his riddle. This constant nagging foreshadows future events where Delilah uses a similar tactic to find the secret of Samson's power: "Finally, after she had nagged him and pressed him constantly, he was wearied to death" (16:16). When Samson reveals the interpretation of the riddle to his wife she tells her people. This is done on the seventh day before sunset. When the sun sets a new day begins, so they gave their answer at the very last minute. Interestingly, the Hebrew Bible uses the poetic word חרסה *ḥarash* for sun, which appears also in Job 9:7. We don't know why the narrator uses this poetic word. BHS proposes חדרה *ḥadrah* 'he entered the room' based on Judges 15:1, which is accepted by NJB. This emendation is too hypothetical as Batrusch noted, the MT is preferable because it builds the suspense toward the end of the story.[11]

Upon receiving the interpretation of the riddle from Samson's wife, the Philistines said to Samson: "What is sweeter than honey and what is stronger than a lion?" Examination of their answer shows that they responded only to the second part of the riddle and not the first part. Samson was not surprised by their answer, he knew that it was his wife who betrayed him and divulged the answer to her people. Evidently, their threat convinced her and she feared them. Samson did not hesitate and immediately responded in poetic form, which comprised of two lines with three words each: "Had you not plowed with my heifer, You would not have guessed my riddle" (v. 18).

Samson fulfilled the terms of his wager and gave a set of clothing to those who answered the riddle, and then returned in rage to his father's

---

11. Bartusch, *Understanding Dan*, 146.

house. We would expect to find Samson angry with the companion before he went to Ashkelon where he killed 30 people. However, the Bible mentions his rage only after he returns from Ashkelon. His anger was directed toward his wife, although, the Bible does not say so explicitly. More so, because of his rage with his wife, he left for his father's house. When Samson left, his father-in-law did not think that Samson would return, therefore, he then gave Samson's wife to one of the companions. Josephus gives a different interpretation. According to him: "but he renounced those nuptials, and the girl, scorning him for his wrath, was united to that friend of his who had given her away."[12] Abravanal goes further and says that Samson's wife behaved like a harlot.

After a while, we are told that Samson remembered his wife and decided to visit her (15:1). This is surprising since she betrayed him by giving away the answer to his riddle. We would expect to read of a break between the two. More so, when Samson responds to the companions, he referred to his wife as a "heifer," which is a disparaging reference. Nevertheless, Samson pursued her with zeal after she was given to another man. After these events, it was "after a while." The precise time is unknown. It may also mean after a year. On that occasion, he brought a kid. It appears that this form of present was a gift among lovers or a form of payment to a harlot. Indeed, it was Judah who sent a kid to Tamar, thinking that she was a harlot. The mention of a kid continues the theme of repeating similar elements that already appeared in the Book of Judges. Hence, as mentioned before Gideon prepared the kid to serve to Yahweh's messenger (6:19); and later Manoah prepared a kid for the angel (13:15, 19).

Samson was under the impression that his marriage was still intact. Therefore, he said to his father-in-law: "Let me go unto my wife, to her room" (v. 1). Evidently, Samson tried to reconcile his marriage with his wife, after a period of separation. Later, a similar scene appears in the Book of Judges when the Levite attempts to reunite with his estranged concubine (19:1–3). Samson does not know that his wife was already given to one of his companions; this piece of information that was divulged to the reader at the end of chapter 14. Thus, his father-in-law refused his request by telling him that she was given to one of the young men from his wedding. He further explained to him that he was certain he hated her, so he gave her to one of the companions. The Hebrew word שׂנא *snʾ* "to hate," which appears

---

12. Josephus, *Ant.* 5.294.

in our text, is a technical term used in matters of divorce (Deut 24:3).[13] Therefore, Bolling concludes that the father-in-law believed that Samson divorced his daughter. Another explanation, following the interpretation of the riddle by the Philistines, is that Samson refers to his wife as a heifer, which belittled her, and then he left quickly. Therefore, his father-in-law thought that Samson hated his daughter so he found her another husband. In other words he thought that Samson would not return to her. The father-in-law took responsibility for the actions of his daughter, and according to Abravanel, he tried to cover up the harlot behavior of his daughter.

The father-in-law found himself in a bad situation because the law in Deuteronomy 24:1 prohibits the return of a wife to her first husband if she had married again. To appease Samson, he offered him his younger daughter. More so, he told him that she was better than her older sister. Malbim explained that he hinted to Samson that she would be more loyal to her husband, and she was prettier than her sister. The story reminds us of a similar scenario that took place many years later when David was supposed to marry the older daughter of King Saul. Merab, Saul's older daughter, was given to Adriel the Meholathite, so instead, the younger daughter Michal was offered to David (1Sam 18:19). A reversal is found in the Jacob cycle, where Jacob had to labor for Rachel, Laban's younger daughter, for seven years, then the older daughter Leah was given to him instead (Gen 29:20–23).

Samson did not accept his father-in-law's offer while speaking to him as well as the other Timnites.[14] Samson had already chosen his own wife and not his parents' choice; to accept his father-in-law's offer was an insult. He felt that no one should accuse him of anything or claim anything from him because of the wrong that was done to him. He decided to take revenge not with his wife or her father but with the Philistines as a whole. Evidently, out of his respect for his wife, he takes no action against her nor her father, but against her people. It is interesting that we don't have any references to his thoughts and feelings about what happened to his wife who was burned by her own people. Hence, it is possible that he did not love her as she told him, "You really hate me, you don't love me" (14:16). As for the Philistines, they burned the Timnite wife and her father as retaliation for Samson burning their crops. They did not retaliate against Samson himself, but against people who were close to him. Ironically, the Timnite

---

13. Bolling, *Judges*, 235.
14. LXX and Vulg read the singular לו *lō* instead of להם *lāhem*.

tries to escape getting burned by cooperating with her own people, the Philistines, to no avail since she is burned by them.

The Harlot from Gaza

The narrative opens with Samson arriving at the city of Gaza where he slept with a harlot. The harlot's name remains anonymous as with the previous Timnite woman that Samson was married to. The women are from two opposite social statuses, the first Timnite woman was Samson's legal wife and this one is a prostitute. The fact that Samson slept with the harlot was the beginning of his downfall. In other words, Samson began to sin in Gaza, therefore, he was punished in Gaza. As noted previously, Samson sinned with his eyes, therefore, his eyes were extracted out.[15] When Samson came to Gaza he "*saw there a harlot*" and he was attracted to her. Radak and Ramban claimed that Samson converted all the women that he engaged with. In contrast, Rashi points out that this woman was not his wife nor did he convert her to Judaism. Hence, it was maintained by the Sages that this affair was his failing and the beginning of his demise. Samson evidently was not looking for love. What we have here is a one night stand; Samson did not even spend the whole night there. To express Samson's sexual desire, the narrator uses the verb בוא *bô'*, "Samson went to Gaza and saw there a harlot and went in to her" (16:1). Interestingly, the narrator already used the verb בוא *bô'* in the Timnite story with the same implications: "I will go in to my wife in the chamber" (15:1). In other words, Samson sought to gratify his sexual urges. Not surprisingly, we are not told of Samson's feelings toward the harlot. No details are given about her, only that she was harlot.

While staying at the home of the harlot, the townspeople planned to ambush and kill Samson. We are not told how they knew that Samson arrived in their city. It is possible that the Gazites heard that he was there. Malbin claims that it was Samson who spread the rumor that he was there. Clearly, Samson was so self-assured in his powers that he was not afraid to come alone to one of the cities of his enemies. Another interpretation is that the harlot betrayed Samson like his first wife who betrayed him and again later with Delilah."[16] Samson is in her house and she knows his whereabouts. In both stories, Samson stays in the woman's house and not in his own house. Both betrayed him for goods. The Timnite woman did

15. b. Soṭah. 9b.
16. Exum, *Fragmented Women Feminist*, 71; Bal, *Lethal Love*, 49.

it because she feared for her life. Although she herself did not receive any goods, it was the companions who received sets of clothing. While the Bible does not mention any form of payment by Samson, the harlot is defined by it. It is noteworthy that although the Tamnite woman is Samson's legal wife, her behavior was immoral like the harlot. Therefore, on his wedding night, Samson charges the companions who 'plowed with my heifer,' which is metaphor for sexual intercourse.[17]

It is not clear why the Philistines decided to kill Samson. Thus, it is possible that the Philistines were aware of his past deeds; therefore, they decided to capture and kill him. The narrator describes how the Philistines gathered and lay waiting in ambush for him the whole night. According to Rashi who follows Targum Jonathan, they conducted themselves quietly. Radak says that they acted like mutes ḥērēš (חרש) so that Samson would not detect them. The narrator uses a range of verbs to describe the activities and preparations of the Philistines to capture Samson, "and they surrounded... and lay in wait for him... they kept quiet... saying, Let us wait till the light of the morning; then we will kill him(16:2)." In other words, the narrator wanted to stress the planning and efforts of the Philistines, which lasted the whole night. Still, if the Philistines were lying and waiting for him all night at the gate of the city, how did Samson pull out the city gate and carry it off unnoticed? Were the Philistines sound sleepers? Or should it read *all day* instead of *all night*?[18] In other words, the gate was closed at night so the Philistines felt that Samson could not escape, thus, they withdrew until morning. It is possible that this note of *all night* is a later edition that came to make Samson escape more heroically.

This story of Samson and the harlot from Gaza is different from Samson's previous story with the Timnite. In that story, the Philistine woman served as a pretext for confrontations and blows against the Philistines. We would expect to read about a new attack against the Philistines, but this does not happen here. Consequently, the reader has to ask himself what the purpose is of Samson going to Gaza. It is possible that Samson expected that the Philistines would try to restore their honor and their attempts will serve as a reason for Samson's attacks. Reading the chapter reveals how Samson was caught by the Philistine's net. The story is a turning point that

---

17. Crenshaw, "Samson Saga," 493–94.
18. Burney, *Judges*, 376; Moore, *Judges*, 349

signals a retreat from the policy of pretext.[19] It serves as an introduction to the last period of Samson's life, which ends with his tragic death.

Samson and Delilah

After leaving Gaza, Samson decided not to endanger Israel, therefore, he sojourned by the brook of Sorek, which is situated along the border of the Philistine territory and Dan. According to the sages, the name *Sorek* "signifies that he had become like a tree which does not yield fruit."[20] This explanation is based on the link between *Sorek* שורק and *Srak* סרק, which is a non-fruit-bearing tree. The story of Samson and Delilah demonstrates that Samson abandoned the divine plan that was set for him. Originally, his actions and deeds were decreed from God. But, his involvement with the harlot showed otherwise, he detaches himself from God's plan. As long as Samson followed the divine plan and killed many Philistines, God was with him. Samson's strength was the result of God's intervention. However, when he did not fulfill the divine plan, he was harmed.

In Samson's previous encounters with women, there is no mention of love. When he married the Timnite woman, the reason for this marriage was because: "she pleases me well" (14:3). In the events that followed his marriage and after his wife was given to another man, there is no declaration of love by Samson. This absence of love is also clear in the story about the harlot. The absence of any emotion on Samson's part suits the divine plan, accordingly, all his actions serve as an excuse to attack the Philistines. The Delilah story, on the other hand, opens with a new twist: the statement that he loved her (16:4). The fact that Samson loved her signals that this time Samson's emotions will play a major roll with his actions leading to his downfall. When the Bible describes love, it uses the root אהב '.*h*.*b* and its derivatives. Its usage is not homogenous. We read of Isaac and Rebekah, Jacob and Rachel, and Elkanah and Hannah, who are all married couples where the husband loves his wife. Michal loved David, but he did not return her love. Ahasuerus loved Esther and Rehoboam loved Maacah; King Solomon loved many women. There are two incidents when love turned to disastrous consequences, when Hamor loved Dinah and Amnon had a passion for his sister. In our story, Samson loved Delilah, but she did not

---

19. Amit, *Judges*, 283.
20. *Num. R.* 9:24.

return his love "for she is but an instrument in a game in which God had something to prove."[21]

Samson loved Delilah, but she is motivated by greed (v.5). To stress this point, the narrator ends this story by saying: "And the lords of the Philistines came up and brought the money with them" (v.18). The story of Samson and Delilah follows the pattern of a wily woman who overpowers a mighty warrior. What is strange in this story is that Samson allowed himself to be deceived for a second time by a woman. We would expect him to learn from his past mistakes.

In contrast to the Timnite and the harlot, the third woman has a name: Delilah. Commenting on her name, the sages say: "Even if her name had not been Delilah she deserved to be called by such a name. She enfeebled his strength, she enfeebled his actions, she enfeebled his determinations."[22] The rabbis explained it based on the root *d.l.l* דלל which means "to weaken," which is part of the name. Strangely enough, Delilah did not live among the Philistines, and therefore, it is not clear if, indeed, she was a Philistine or might have been an Israelite or a Canaanite woman. There is no mention of the city that she lived in, but the name of the wadi is mentioned: Sorek. This place is identified with a modern wadi eṣ-Ṣarâr on the northern edge of which Zorah is situated. In other words, the Sorek valley bordered Danite and Philistines territories. Delilah has her own house and has ties to the Philistine chiefs. Since Samson went after non-Israelites, it is more likely that he also continued with this pattern, therefore, Delilah must have been a Philistine.

The story of Samson and Delilah is modeled on a numerical arrangement of three and four. This kind of pattern is found in persuasion attempts. Indeed, it appears already in the attempt to persuade the thorn bush to reign (Judg 9:8–15). Three times Delilah attempted to find the secret of Samson's powers. The first time she tied him with seven fresh tendons that had not been dried (16:6–9). The second time she bound him with new ropes that had never been used (vv.10–12). The third time she wove the seven locks of his head into the web (vv.13–14). On the last and fourth time, Samson reveals to Delilah the secret of his powers that caused his downfall (vv.15–21). Three times Samson used his special strength for his own needs and not for fighting the Philistines. Not surprisingly, he failed during the fourth time. Scholars are at odds as to the purpose of this model. According

---

21. Sasson, "Who Cut Samson Hair?" 334–35.
22. *b. Soṭah.* 9b.

to Blenkinsopp, it points to the different stages in the story development.[23] Zakovitch, on the other hand, maintains that this model served the needs of persuasion.[24]

It is noteworthy that Delilah tied Samson three times, which has a similarity to the incident in Ramath–lehi. As the reader recalls in that episode, the man of Judah bound Samson with two new ropes (15:13). Nevertheless, the comparison between these two events shows the glaring contrast between them. At Ramath-lehi Samson used his divine powers to save himself and to slay many Philistines. In this story, Samson uses his divine powers as part of his love play with Delilah: he was teasing her.[25] He did not use his power against the Philistines and, therefore, he failed.

Delilah asked Samson the secret of his strength. Her question is forthright and direct; she wants to know how he can be overpowered. In response, Samson answered: "If I were to be tied with seven fresh tendons that had not been dried, I should become as weak as an ordinary man"(16:7). Samson replies with a lie: it appears that he understood the reason for Delilah's question. The phrase, 'I should become as an ordinary man,' and the number seven will be repeated in the other attempts of Delilah to find Samson's secret. All along Delilah is working closely with the Philistines who came and brought her seven fresh tendons that had not been dried. When Delilah binds Samson, the Philistines were waiting in her room to capture him. She tells Samson, 'The Philistines are upon you Samson,' a phrase that she will repeat three more times. As expected, Samson snaps the cords and Delilah's first attempt is a failure. Samson continues to hide the secret of his strength, while Delilah continues to collaborate with the Philistines to find the secret of Samson's strength.

Since Delilah failed to discover Samson's secret, she accuses Samson of mocking her by telling her lies. In other words, she implies that he is unfaithful to her. She asks him how he can be tied up. This time, the text does not mention any reference to torment. Samson does not respond to her accusation, instead he tells her that if he were to be tied up with new ropes, he would become as weak as an ordinary man. Again, Samson gives a similar answer that repeats his first. Instead of seven fresh tendons, this time it is new ropes however, nothing is said about the number of ropes. Although Samson was tied before, it appears that Delilah believed him, but

---

23. Blenkinsopp, "Structure and Style," 74.
24. Zakovitch, *Life of Samson*, 171.
25. Amit, *Judges*, 286.

again we have the same result. Samson snaps the ropes off his arms like a thread. Meanwhile, the Philistine ambush was waiting in the room. It is strange that Samson hears Delilah call upon the Philistines repeatedly (vv.9, 12, 14, 20), and in the end, he still divulged his secret.

In the third attempt to find Samson's secret, there is a change. Samson is closer to revealing the source of strength. For the first time Samson mentions his hair, which is the true source of his strength. He refers to his seven locks of his head hair. This is the first time that we read that Samson wears his hair in seven locks. Mentioning seven locks suggests that he took care to maintain it. Before, Samson's hair was loose and not bound. Here for the first time, it is the locks of his head hair that are bound. Samson tells Delilah to weave the seven locks of his hair into a web and fasten it with the pin. This time she puts him to sleep. It appears as though he trusts her. As before, she is calling upon the Philistines but again with the same results; Samson pulled out the peg, the loom, and the web.

Despite her previous failure to find the secret of Samson's strength, Delilah continued with relentless zeal. This probably lasted for some time since each time she puts him to sleep. Moreover, in her fourth attempt, we read that it lasted for seven days. She blamed him for being untruthful with her and three times he deceived her, so his love for her is also unreal. She uses a guilt trip here, juxtaposing love and secret together. If Samson loves her, he will reveal to her his secret. We find out that she started לענותו *l'noto* "made him helpless." This verb already appears when the Philistines state that their intention is to imprison and abuse Samson. It is used here by Delilah when she tries to find Samson's secret (v.7). Besides nagging him, she also pressed him *wt'lṣhw* (ותאלצהו). According to Rashi, there is no similar word in the Scripture. The sages raised the question, "What could Delilah do to cause Samson distress?" They answered this by suggesting, "At the time of the culmination of cohabitation, she would slip away from beneath him."[26] Samson was in such distress that he was exasperated to the point of death. This description is similar to the fleeing of Elijah (1Kgs 19:4) and Jonah (4:8), where those prophets were so frustrated with God that they requested to die.[27] What is not clear is why Samson did not leave her. Instead, he stayed and was under continuous pressure. This leads us back to verse 4 where we read that he loved her.

---

26. b. Soṭah. 9b.
27. Boling, *Judges*, 250.

When Delilah tries for the first time to find Samson's secret, she asks him three questions: 1. "What makes you strong?" 2. "What would bind you?" 3. "What would weaken you?" Interestingly, these three components are not mentioned again. In the second and third attempts only "what would bind you?" is mentioned. While in the fourth attempt, it is "what makes you strong?"[28]

In reveling his secret to Delilah, Samson repeated the instructions that were given by the angel (Judg13:5). He tells Delilah the secret of his Nazirite status, and by doing so, he exposed himself to the loss of his powers. This time, Delilah knew that he told her the truth. The sages asked how she knew. They offered two explanations: first, true words are recognizable and second, "She knew about the righteous one that he would not utter the name of Heaven in vain. Hence, as soon as he said: I am a *nazir* to God, she said to herself, 'Now he is certainly telling the truth.'"[29] Another explanation was offered by Rashi who maintained that she was convinced of the truth of his statement by his appearance and his conduct. She saw his long hair and she knew that he never drank wine.

Compared to the last two times when the lords of the Philistines were not present, this time they arrived at the house of Delilah. More so, they brought the money with them. According to Abravanel, they brought the money because she assured them that she knew the truth. While putting Samson to sleep upon her knees, she called the man who assisted her in shaving Samson. The Philistines probably also brought her the razor. The man evidently shaved Samson under her instructions. It is possible that she was afraid that he would wake up, therefore, she needed the assistance of a man. While Samson was shaved, we read that at this stage she began to afflict him and his strength left him (16:19). Radak explains that although he was asleep, he felt his strength departing from him and was thereby afflicted. Alternatively, she tied him up. Another explanation given was that the shaving began the process of suffering. Delilah was responsible for the start of his pain, which would be continued by the Philistines. Delilah does what the Philistines already planned to do to Samson, "tie him up, and make him helpless" (v.5). The LXX, on the other hand, translated that it was the Philistines who started to afflict him.

As before, Delilah calls "Samson, the Philistines are upon you." Samson woke up from his sleep. He thought that he could break loose and shake

---

28. Sasoon, "Who Cut Samson's Hair?" 335.
29. b. Soṭah. 9b.

himself free as he had done the other three times. It appears he was drowsy at the time. Samson forgot that he told Delilah the secret of his power and did not realize what had transpired. Or, he still did not notice that his hair was shaven, therefore, he did not know that the Lord departed from him. He thought that God, as before, would assist him against the Philistines. But not this time. The Philistines seized him and gouged his eyes, thus, assuring themselves that he could not harm them anymore. They did not kill him, but they punished him severely as they told the people of Judah. Their intention was to humiliate him over a period of time.

Conclusion

Three women are mentioned in the Samson stories. Each represents a different kind of relationship with Samson. The women were all foreigners, Philistines. The first two women, the Timnite and the harlot, are nameless. The third woman is given the name Delilah. The first relationship with the Timnite was allegedly as a result of physical attraction, "she is right in my eyes," but it was from God. Samson does not exhibit any emotions toward her during her life and following her death. She serves as a reason for killing the Philistines. The second one is the harlot from Gaza who represents lust. The lust story is the beginning of Samson's downfall, which leads us to the Delilah story and to the tragic death of Samson. The third woman, Delilah represents love. We are told that Samson loved her, but Delilah loved money and betrayed Samson.

Both the Timnite and Delilah yielded to the pressure of their own people and both betrayed Samson. The Philistines used women to obtain knowledge. The three foreign women who appear in the Samson stories are bad ones as they are the subject of Samson's sexual desire. The stories display Samson's attraction to foreign women who have the upper hand, so they are on the victorious side. The women serve as glue to the whole Samson saga. Without them, there is no story. Samson's involvement with them puts the stories into motion and leads Samson to fight continuously with the Philistines. But, all of this involvement with the foreign women was not a coincidence, as we are told at the beginning of the story: "His father and mother did not realize that this was the Lord's doing: He was seeking a pretext against the Philistines, for the Philistines were ruling over Israel at that time" (Judg 14:4).

The Samson Story

During the festivities celebrating his marriage, Samson entertains the Philistines with a riddle challenging them to solve it. The next chapter examines the subject of Samson's riddle, the Philistines' riddle, and riddles in the Hebrew Bible.

5

Samson's Riddle

DURING THE FESTIVITIES CELEBRATING his marriage, Samson presents the Philistines with a riddle and challenges them to solve it within the seven days of the wedding celebrations. If they succeed in solving his riddle, he will provide them with 30 linen tunics and 30 sets of clothing. However, if they fail, they must give him 30 linen tunics and 30 sets of clothing. In the ancient world, the riddle was a source of entertainment, especially at banquets and celebrations in the king's court. It was a test of wisdom. This chapter will examine the subject of riddles in the Hebrew Bible. In addition, we will look into the details of Samson's riddle. Scholars maintain that Samson's riddle is independent and not connected to the narrative. Both the riddle and the answer are older than this story, which prompted the creation of the story of the slain lion and eating the honey from the lion's skeleton. Hence, we will survey the different proposals and solutions. We will also study the Philistine's answer to Samson's riddle. Did they indeed offer an interpretation to his riddle? Did their response have any link to the riddle itself? Was it an answer to the riddle or was it a question? Finally, we will look into Samson's response to the Philistines to understand what stands behind his words, which are narrated in such a poetic form.

Riddles in the Hebrew Bible

The Hebrew word חידה *ḥidah* (riddle) is derived from a root denoting *hidden thing*. This was a source of entertainment in the ancient world, especially at banquets and celebrations at the kings court (1kgs 10:1; Ezek 17:2). The bards, the reciters of משלים *meshalim*, were known for specializing in a literary form of proverb, parable, or riddle (Num 21:27). The Septuagint renders the Hebrew term *ḥidah* as "those who speak in enigma." Most well-known is the "war of riddles" at the court of the king of Babylon, where Zerubbabel defeats the advisers of the king and received praises and glory for it (I Esdras 3: 13–41). The riddle was also a test of wisdom. King Solomon was known for his wisdom and his ability to solve riddles: "The queen of Sheba heard of Solomon's fame—through the name of the Lord, and she came to test him with hard questions חידות (*ḥidot*)" (1Kgs 10:1). As expected, Solomon answered all her questions so she saw all his wisdom. Solomon and riddles are also mentioned in Josephus's writings. He mentions an exchange of riddles between Solomon and Hiram the king of Tyre:

> "And they say that Solomon, who was tyrant of Jerusalem, sent riddles to Eirōmos and asked to receive others from him as well, proposing that he who was unable to interpret them should pay a fine to the one who did solve them. But Eirōmos, having agreed to this was unable to solve the riddles paid out large sums of money as a fine. Afterwards through a certain Abdēmon a Tyrian citizen, he solved the riddles proposed and himself offered others, which Solomon was unable to solve and paid large sums to Eirōmos in return."[1]

Another king who was known to solve riddles is mentioned in a vision that was given to Daniel. Accordingly, at the end of the four kingdoms: " . . . then a king will rise, impudent and versed in intrigue חידות (*ḥidot*)," (Dan 8:23). Understanding riddles is one of the traits of a wise man, hence, we read in the Book of Proverbs: "For understanding proverb and epigram, The words of the wise and their riddles . . . " (Prov 1:5–6). The fact that riddles are words of wisdom is also mentioned in the Book of Psalms where the words, proverbs, and riddles are juxtaposed (Ps 49:5). The narrator mentions that playing the lyre will serve as inspiration for solving the riddle. Proverbs and riddles are mentioned side by side again in Psalms 78:2. The riddles are characterized as lessons of the past: " . . . things we have heard and known, that our fathers have told us."

The prophets used riddles as a form of communication. God instructed Ezekiel to propose a riddle (Ezek 17:1). In his riddle and proverb, he describes an eagle and a cedar tree, which refers to the people of Israel. The prophet used this literary form because he could not speak freely. He lived in exile, and the use of this genre is a well-known technique that is used by authors, poets, and leaders who lived under oppressive regimes. It's

---

1. Josephus, *Antq*, 8.148–49.

not clear from whom the prophet is afraid. He is also very careful when he reveals the riddle (vv.11–18), so it was probably done privately and not in public. In the interpretation, he mentions Babylon and Egypt but not the names of the kings of Babylon nor the king of Judah. It is possible that he was cautious because he feared that the Babylonians would use his words against the deserters from Zedkiau army and blame them for disloyalty.

Prophets would solve visions that God revealed to them. It is believed that many prophetic utterances, although not labelled as riddles, are riddles because they have the same format.[2] In other words, they were developed from the riddle. A good example is the vision that Amos received: "What do you see, Amos? I said a lump of tin. My Lord said soon I will put grief in the midst of my people Israel. I shall not spare them again" (7:8). Similarly, in the Book of Jeremiah: "What do you see? I replied: I see a steaming pot, tipped away from north. And the Lord said to me: From the north shall disaster break loose upon all the inhabitants of the land" (1:13). When Jeremiah sees an almond tree שָׁקֵד (shaqed), the answer he received is in the form of a riddle by means of paronomasia: "For I am watchful שֹׁקֵד (shoked) to bring My word to pass" (vv.11–12).

It is not only the prophets who communicated with the people of Israel through riddles. God used a riddle to reveal himself. When God spoke about Moses as a unique prophet He said: "With him I speak mouth to mouth, in a vision and not riddles, and he beholds the likeness of the Lord" (Num 12:8). Expounding on Moses as a unique prophet, Rabbi Judah says:

> 'All the prophets saw through nine mirrors, as it is written, "like the vision of the vision I had seen, like the vision I had seen when I came to destroy the city, and visions like the vision that I had seen by the Chebar Canal. Forthwith, I fell on my face" (Ezek 43:3). But Moses saw through only one mirror—in a vision and not in riddles" (Num 12:8)' Our sages say that all the prophets saw through a clouded mirror, as it say, 'When I spoke to the prophets, I granted many visions [and spoke parables through the prophets]'(Hos 12:11).[3]

This homily is based on the principle that prophetic sight is like looking in a mirror that distorts the image somewhat. Moses looked through only a single mirror, whereas the other prophets saw an image that had been reflected nine times, so that the image was greatly distorted. In other

2. Blank, "Riddle," 4:79
3. *Lev. R. 1:14.*

words, Moses does not need any interpretation, but the visions, dreams, or riddles of the other prophets do.

Interestingly when Moses asked for God's name, the answer that he received is in the form of a riddle: אהיה אשר אהיה "*Ehyeh–Asher Ehyeh*" (Exod 3:14), which has been variously translated as, "I Am That I Am," "I Am Who I Am," and "I Will Be What I Will Be."

Hints of riddles are also found in the symbolic dreams in the Hebrew Bible. These types of dreams required the aid of an interpreter of dreams who deciphered the symbols in the dreams. This category includes the dreams of the Butler and the Baker, which Joseph interpreted. Pharaoh's two dreams are also mentioned where the magician failed to interpret but Joseph successfully deduced.[4] A form of a riddle is mentioned in the dream of a Midianite man who described a loaf of barley bread was whirling through the Midianite camp (Judg 7:13). The dream evidently refers to the ensuing attack against the Midianite camp by Gideon.

Samson's Riddle

During the festivities celebrating his marriage Samson entertained the Philistines with a riddle and challenged them to solve it within seven days of the wedding celebrations. Should they solve his riddle, he would provide them with 30 linen tunics and 30 sets of clothing.[5] However, if they could not solve it they must give him 30 linen tunics and 30 sets of clothing. The Philistines accepted Samson's challenge and asked him to narrate his riddle. As is known, Samson's riddle was based on his adventure with the lion. "So he said to them:

> "Out of the eater came something to eat,
>
> מהאכל יצא מאכל
>
> *mh'kl yṣ' m'kl*
>
> Out of the strong came something sweet" (Judg 14:14).

---

4. For the subject of dream interpretation in the Hebrew Bible see: Bar, *A letter that Has Not Been Read*, 78–107

5. The linen garments that Samson promised are mentioned in Isaiah 3:23 and Proverbs 31:24. It was made of fine linen and it was worn as undergarment next to the body or as an outer robe to cover the clothes. The change of raiment Hebrew חליפות *ḥaliphoth* refers to festive garments in contrast to working grab. It was given as a mark of favor (Gen 45: 22; 2Kgs 5:5, 22).

Samson's Riddle

ומעז יצא מתוק
wm'z yṣ' mtwq

The riddle appears in short poetic form and is arranged in two parallel lines containing three Hebrew words in each line. The riddle describes Samson's two trips to Timnah. The word *strong* in line two refers to his first trip and his struggle with the *lion*, while the word *sweet* refers to his second trip, where he found the honey in the carcass of the lion. The first line uses the same Hebrew word (אכל) *'kl* out of the *eater* came something to *eat*. At first glance, it appears to be a contradiction, since an eater consumes food and does not produce food. The first and second lines use the verb יצא *yṣ'*, which creates a parallelism between the two lines. The second line contains two adjectives עז *'z* and מתוק *mtwq*, which correspond to the two objects of the stich. In other words, *eater* refers to *strong* and *food* to *sweet*. Hence, the answer to the riddle should be concentrated on the two words strong עז *'z* and sweet מתוק *mtwq*.

The connection between the two trips is noted in the Midrash. According to the sages, Samson thought of the riddle while eating honey: "Samson was wondering in his heart, saying to himself: The lion eats all animals, and now the food comes out of him!"[6] Hence, if the riddle was indeed linked to his past travels, it was impossible to solve the riddle if the story was unknown. The word "eater" does not necessarily refer to a lion, although in some instances, the verb is linked to lions (1Kgs 13:28; Jer 2:30); while the adjective "strong" speaks of other animals in a negative way (Prov 30:25). As for the word "food," it does not specifically denote honey. On the other hand, the word "sweet" appears as describing honey (Ezek 3:3; Ps 19:11; Prov 24:13). Still, it was a difficult task to solve the riddle when given only one word. Moore points out: "It was, in truth, a very bad riddle, and quite insoluble without a knowledge of the accidental circumstance which suggested it."[7] Moore raises the question as to the fairness of making such a query of the Philistines, asking whether we can count this as a riddle. Samson's unfair riddle evidently troubled Malbim, who took an innovative approach. According to him, Samson told the Philistines to search around the city to discover the solution to the riddle. In other words, Samson was referring to the lion's carcass.

It was suggested to eliminate the idea of the "riddle" and to explain the story as part of the myth cycle about a Sun-Hero, which has a parallel

---

6. *Lev. Rabba.* 8:2.
7. Moore, *Judges*, 335.

The Samson Story

in ancient mythology.[8] A well-known story quoted by Virgil tells about Aristeas; his bees abandoned him so he sacrificed oxen to Zeus, who in return, sent him a new swarm. Another story is about Onesilaus, in whose skull bees hived.[9] As pointed out, the Greek myth speaks of skull or an ox's carcass, while the Bible speaks about a lion.[10] The comparison between Samson and the Sun-Hero is not convincing (see in next chapter). The fact that bees don't hive in carcasses is also disputed. It is believed that bees can hive in carcasses after the smell of decay dissipates, which usually takes a year. According to the biblical text, Samson went for the second time to see his wife to be, "Sometime later, in the season of the wheat harvest" (Judg 15:1). This implies a year passed by in which nothing was left of the carcass; it disintegrated. The wedding took place at the season of the wheat harvest, which means the winter rains washed and cleaned the carcass. This harvest season was also suitable for the bees to produce honey that Samson ate and also gave to his parents.[11]

Attempts were also made to explain the symbols in the riddle in an astrological way. The bees produced honey in the lion, the month the sun stands in the sign of Leo (the Lion). This explanation tries to harmonize the terms lion and honey. Accordingly, it would be reasonable for an ancient riddle to offer a paradox. However, the original meaning of the riddle has been eliminated in the Samson story as the redactor concealed other mythological references.[12]

A different approach was taken by Margalith and Yadin who cited Greek traditions. The Philistines, who came from the Minoan-Mycenean culture, were familiar with the story of Aristaeus. According to Margalith, so was Samson. Therefore, he was able to offer a riddle that is based on bees and a lion carcass. The storyteller and the audience were also familiar with the Greek traditions.[13] Strangely enough, the Philistines could not come up with the solution, and only after pressuring Samson's wife did they came up with the right answer. Yadin follows Maraglith's assumption that the Greek culture is key to understanding the wedding narrative. The journey to the house of the bride and the banquet at the house of the bride's father are

---

8. Margalith, "Samson's Riddle," 227
9. Virgil, *Georgics*, iv: 299–315, 555–58.
10. Margalith, "Samson's Riddle," 227
11. Samueli, "Samson's Riddle," 58.
12. Carus, *Story of Samson*, 92.
13. Margalith, "Samson's Riddle," 228–29

typically Greek customs. Wedding feasts were followed by a ceremony in which the groom unveiled the bride, followed by the consummation of the marriage in the bridal chambers. However, Samson left his bride's house without consummating the marriage, therefore, she was not his wife although she is referred as such (v. 16).[14] This might explain why she was given to someone else. According to Yadin, the exchange between Samson and the Philistines is called a Greek *skolion*. Capping songs was a well-known custom where invited guests improvised verses at the wedding.[15] The most common technique involved the contender reciting the first verse of the poem and the other guests were supposed to give the second, third, and fourth verses and so on. This is why the Philistines reply is inexplicable, they came with their own riddle, not with a solution to Samson's riddle. The riddle itself alludes to a fable concerning honey and a lion based on cultural knowledge. The Philistines explained it as love or sexual desire.[16] However, Philistines maintaining Greek customs is unproven. It also eliminates the connections between 14:5–9 and the wedding narrative.[17] It is not clear if Samson himself was familiar with Greek culture.

Other scholars offered different interpretations. Herzberg, for example, suggests that the riddle refers metaphorically to male potency.[18] Hence, מהאכל *mh'kl* eater refers to the lion as the bridegroom while מאכל *m'kl* food or the honey as the male sperm. On the other hand, עז *'z* strong and מתוק *mtwq* sweet show the quality of love. Eissfeldt explains the riddle in a similar way but claims that vv.14 and 18 are two separate riddles. According to him, "eat" and "drink" metaphorically describe sexual intercourse. The answer to the first riddle was so ill-mannered that it was omitted by later traditions.[19] While, Gressman proposed that the riddle is about a man who eats and drinks heavily at the banquet and as a result, vomits.[20] This, according to Grassmen was appropriate for a marriage feast. The problem with this interpretation was that it only relates to the riddle, while it ignores the interpretation. More so the suggestion that it refers to the vomiting of food is unacceptable simply because vomit is not food for nourishment for

---

14. Yadin, "Samson's Ḥîdâ," 419.
15. Ibid.
16. Ibid., 422.
17. Butler, *Judges*, 337.
18. Hertzberg, *Die Bücher Josua, Richter, Ruth*, 230.
19. Eissfeldt, "Die Rätsel in Jud 14," 134.
20. Gressmann, *Die Anfänge Israels*, 244.

others. The word *food* in our verse refers both to food and sweets, which is honey.

Gaster suggested that the answer to the riddle is honey:

> *It comes from "the eater"*
> *'this something you eat.*
> *—from something fierce*
> *but itself is sweet.*[21]

This explanation has difficulties with v.18 "What is stronger than a lion?" Hence, it was Bauer who pointed out that the word *'ry* appears in Arabic with the meaning "honey." In other words, *'ry* means both lion and honey.[22] Originally, it was a linguistic riddle based on two words with the same meaning.[23] The word initially was in the first line of the distich in 18a, forming a pun on the Hebrew word ארי *'ry* lion in the second line. Later, when one of the meanings was lost, it was replaced with the familiar word דבש *debash*[24] While the meaning honey in Arabic was preserved in Hebrew, only the verb is found. In Song of Songs, the author says: "I plucked (*'ry*) my myrrh with my spice; I ate my honeycomb with my honey" (5:1). It is possible that the biblical description was influenced by this similar double meaning. Segert, who follows Bauer's explanation, says that since the word for honey and lion are the same, the riddle had to be solved by finding a pair of homonyms; one that means something strong, the other meaning something sweet. According to him, it was not essential to know what Samson did with the lion since nobody saw him.[25] If the riddle was a wordplay and did not have a connection with Samson killing the lion, the question needed to be asked as to why the Philistines could not solve the riddle. As mentioned above, it is possible that the meaning of *'ry* as honey was not prevalent anymore, and only the meaning of lion was preserved. Hence, the wordplay that was employed by Samson was an enigma to the Philistines. Since the original meaning was lost, it was thought that the riddle was connected to some act that was performed by Samson that involved a lion and the honey, and it became the subject of the riddle as well

---

21. Gaster, *Myth Legend*, 436.
22. Bauer, "Zu Simsons Rätsel," 473–74; Kopf, "Honey," 240–42.
23. Bauer, "Zu Simsons Rätsel," 473–74.
24. Porter "Samson's Riddle," 106–09.
25. Segert, "Paronomasia," 456.

as its solution.[26] It is also possible that the Philistines did not speak Hebrew well or spoke a different dialect. The Hebrew language had several dialects, one of which the Philistines used where the word *'ry* meaning honey did not exist.[27]

Alternatively, the words 'out of the eater' and 'strong' do not necessarily refer to a lion. Similarly, the words 'to eat' and 'sweet' are not necessarily referring to honey. Therefore, it is possible the riddle could also refer to a bee; her sting is fierce and she produces sweet food. However, it appears that our riddle is connected to past events and the other solutions suggested have no strong ties to our story.

Samson was confident the Philistines would fail in their attempt to solve his riddle. He set a trap and acted in a dishonest way. Thus, not surprisingly he took a big wager. Still, we have to remember that deception was a way of life in the ancient world. In the Jacob cycle, trickery and deception is one of the main motifs. All protagonists take part and play a role in deception: Jacob, Rebecca, Laban, Leah, Rachel, Simeon and Levi, Hamor and his son Shechem, Jacob's sons, as well as Tamar, Judah's daughter-in-law. The motif of deception is also found in Greek literature, where humans and gods deceive each other. Athena is dressing herself up as an old man. Penelope lies about Laertes's magically shrinking shroud. Odysseus is the king of lies. As for the gods, they too deceive all the time. The aim of these deceptions was to gain the advantage of being in control.

The Philistines' Riddle

The Philistines presented their answer to the riddle:

"What is sweeter than honey

מה מתוק מדבש

mh-mtwq mdbš

and what is stronger than a lion."

ומה עז מארי

wmh 'z m'ry

26. Sameuli, "Samson's Riddle," 61.
27. Ibid.

The Philistines answered in 2+ 2 poetic parallelism. Each of their statements begins in question form: מה *mh* (what). In the Hebrew Bible the narrator often uses an interrogative form and gives the answer this way. These two lines constructed in poetic parallelism are similar to the two lines of Samson's riddle. Instead of answering Samson's riddle, the Philistines tease Samson with their own riddle. According to Abravanel they answered indirectly to imply they discovered the solution upon their own investigation. The implication is that even a fool could solve the riddle. Examination of their answer shows that they responded only to the second part of the riddle and not the first part. They explain "strong" and "sweet" but not "eater" and "food." As a matter of fact it is not really an answer to the riddle, it is a question.

At first glance, Samson's riddle and its interpretation are keeping with one another and they matched the events narrated in the story. However, a close examination reveals that there are difficulties in the text. Hence, Gunkel came to the conclusion that the riddle has not come to us in its original form. Gressmann who follows Gunkel's lead, says: "one is especially astonished at the answer of Samson's companions, 'what is sweeter than honey and what is more voracious than a lion?' Hence, the words "sweet" and "voracious" refer to the riddle, while the words honey and lion allude to Samson's experience. According to the narrator, the solution to the riddle is linked to events of Samson's life. The sentence is constructed as a rhetorical question in the declarative form: 'Nothing is sweeter than honey, and nothing is more voracious than a lion.' However, according to the content of the story, the answer that we should expect would have to read 'honey came forth from the lion.' This is the answer that the narrator had in mind, but he preferred the poetic style to dry prose. Hence, it is believed that we have here a "quotation," which gives the solution in a clever way. [28]

The answer the Philistines gave in interrogatory form suggests that we have here a second riddle: "What can be sweeter than honey and what can be more voracious than a lion.' Thus, Gunkel advocated that the riddle speaks about love, which is stronger than a lion and sweeter than honey.[29] This solution is more suitable to the companion's interpretation and not to Samson's riddle. The 'love answer' would fit the setting of the marriage feast. The only connection between the two riddles is the wedding festival.[30] The

---

28. Gressmann, *Die Anfänge Israels*, 243; Tur-Sinai, "Riddle," 62.
29. Gunkel, 'Simson,' 53
30. Gressmann, *Die Anfänge Israels*, 244.

words "sweetens" and "strongest" allude to love, power, and ecstasy. Gunkel translated עז ʿz in 14:18 as 'bitter's 'geirig' based on Isaiah 56:11, Eccls 6:4; 19:3, and 40:30. However, this meaning of עז ʿz has not been supported. To bolster his argument, he compared the riddle to similar metaphors in Song of Songs: "for love is as strong as death, jealousy is as cruel as the grave (8:6)." According to him, only love can be described as sweet and bitter.[31] Thus, according to Gunkel:

> "The angels call it heavenly joy,
> The demons call it hellish grief,
> By men it love is called.
> O love, how bitter art thou,
> O love, how sweet thou art.'

Nel also maintains that the solution to the riddle is love. The wedding setting is a hint in that direction since love enjoys a certain priority at the feast. He suggests that the solution existed as a popular proverb. More so, "it is possible that this saying was originally a folklorist riddle."[32] According to him, well-known riddles gained for themselves the status of proverbs. The subject of this proverb is love. The two key words "sweet" and "strong" refer to love. The answer to Samson's riddle is the popular proverb (v.18), where those words play a central role. Hence, v.18 is the solution to the riddle.

Block maintains that based on contextual grounds, the answer is linked to the wedding. Line one refers to love, which is incomparable in its sweetness, while line two refers to Samson, who is known for his strength. Nevertheless, love proved to be stronger. According to him: "from the narrator's perspective, despite Samson's great physical strength and the force of his Nazirite vow, he is completely helpless when confronted with the love of women. From Yahweh's prospective the amorous desires of this man provide the occasions for the beginning of the conflict between Samson and the Philistines."[33]

Samson's Reply

Samson appears to accept the Philistines answer as correct. Their response did not mislead Samson who responded to them. Although at first he was

---

31. Gunkel, "Simson," 54–55.
32. Nel, "Riddle of Samson," 542.
33. Block, *Judges, Ruth*, 435

surprised at their answer, he immediately responded in poetic form, which comprised of two lines with three Hebrew words each:

"Had you not plowed with my heifer,

lwl' ḥrštm b'glty

לולא חרשתם בעגלתי

You would not have guessed my riddle" (v. 18).

l' mṣ'tm ḥydty

לא מצאתם חידתי

The first line is taken from the world of farmers; he refers to his wife allegorically as a heifer and the companions as the one who used her for plowing. In other words, through Samson's wife, they discovered his thoughts. He blamed the companions, not his wife. Some suggest that the use of the term "heifer" for his wife is disparaging.[34] Ralbag (Acronym for Rabbi Levi ben Gershom, known as Gersonides, 1288–1344) suggested that Samson's wife divulged the secret to the Philistines, and Samson was suspicious that she slept with one of them, and then revealed the secret of the riddle. However, it was because of their threats that she responded to them. Nevertheless, Samson indirectly prophesied since she was later given to one of the companions. Following the theme of love and sexuality, which was the subject of the Philistines' answer (riddle), we might say that his answer was a description of a sexual act. Indeed, in the cultures of the Ancient Near East, the metaphor of plowing is used to describe sexual acts. A letter from Rib-Addi of Byblos reads: "My field is like a woman without a husband, on account of its lack of cultivation."[35] The metaphorical usage of "plowing" to describe sexual intercourse is also found in rabbinic literature. In *y. Yebam* 1.1.2b, it says that Rabbi Yossi, son of Ḥalafta married his brother's wife in a levirate marriage: "He plowed five plowings, had intercourse through a sheet, and planted five plantings [sired five sons]."[36] Webb suggests that plowing has a double service, both an agricultural as well as a sexual metaphor.[37] According

---

34. Ibid., 435–36.
35. Pfeifer, "Akkadian Proverbs," In *ANET*, 426.
36. Paul, "Plowing with a Heifer," 163–67.
37. Webb, *Judges*, 374.

to Crenshaw: "Samson's defeat comes because his wife performed the task of an animal. Later, Samson will himself carry out the work of oxen."[38]

Samson paid the garments he promised the Philistines, although he knew they deceived him. He accused the Philistines of "plowing with his heifer." Thus, in return, he deceived them by killing 30 Philistines in Ashkelon and taking their garments.

Conclusion

In the Hebrew Bible as well as in the ancient world, the riddle was a source of entertainment, especially at banquets and celebrations in a king's court; it was a test of wisdom. Many of the prophetic sayings and some of the dreams in the Bible have the form of a riddle. More so, it was one of the ways that God thought to reveal himself. Samson's riddle is at the core of chapter 14, and its serves as a bridge to the ensuing events. With the Philistines solving the riddle, it was the beginning of Samson's retaliatory acts. Those acts would go back and forth until his death. Many suggestions were given as to the source of Samson's riddle. It was thought that both the riddle and its answer are older than the Samson narrative and prompted the creation of the story of the slain lion and eating the honey from its carcass. Alternatively, some say the riddle is based on an old saying that was interlaced into the Samson narrative, saying that was appropriate at a wedding feast. This and other suggestions are very interesting, but they are mere speculation and not convincing. Samson's riddle in its current form is based on his adventure with the lion. The riddle describes to us his two trips to Timnah. In his first trip, he killed a lion and in the second he ate honey from the carcass of the lion. The Philistines answered Samson's riddle indirectly to imply that they discovered the solution on their own. Their answer shows that they responded only to the second part of the riddle and not the first part. They explain "strong" and "sweetens" but not "eater" and "food." Samson never questioned their interpretation, he just accepted it. Their response did not mislead him. He knew that it was his wife who gave the Philistines the interpretation to the riddle, because he alluded to it in his response to them. The next chapter will continue with the theme of Samson's heroic actions. Thus, we will examine the mythological elements that are connected to his actions.

---

38. Crenshaw, *Samson*, 119.

6

Mythical Elements in the Samson Story

MYTHS ARE STORIES ABOUT gods or other superhuman beings, which are told to explain a custom, institution or natural phenomenon. Direct parallels between the Hebrew Bible and the Ancient Near Eastern myths are found in the story of Yahweh fighting the dragon, the stories of creation, and the tale of the deluge. Residue of myths is also found in biblical poetry: the wind has wings (1Sam 22:11; Hos 4:19); thunder is the Lord's voice (2Sam 22:14); and the Lord rides clouds (Ps 68:5). The religion of Israel is unfavorable to myths because it is a monotheistic religion. Nevertheless, the writers of the Hebrew Bible sometimes used mythical elements in their writings to accommodate their own perceptions.

Among the different types of myths, one form that can be found in the Hebrew Bible is the hero myth. Traces of the ancient Hebrew hero myth are apparent to one reading the story about Enoch (Gen 5:24). This Enoch tradition has a parallel in Mesopotamian mythology, in the figure of Enmeduranki, the seventh king of the antediluvian Sipar.[1] Sipar was a center of the cult of the sun god Utu.[2] The gods welcomed him into their midst, revealed their secrets to him, seated him on a golden throne, and initiated him in the practice of divination. The Mesopotamian myth links this king to the sun god, who presides over the 365-day solar year, just as Enoch's Biblical life span is 365 years. The Babylonian king was the seventh in the antediluvian line, just as Enoch is the seventh generation from Adam.[3] The king is intimate with the gods, just as Enoch "walked with God" (Gen 5:24).

1. Jacobson, *Sumerian King List*, 75; Vander Kam, *Enoch*, 33–51.
2. Skinner, *Genesis*, 132; Achard, *From Death to Life*, 68; Speiser, *Genesis*, 43.
3. Lambert, "Enmeduranki," 126–38; Sasson, "A Genealogical 'Convention,'" 171–85.

Another hero that is mentioned in the Hebrew Bible is Nimrod. He is described in the Table of Nations as "a mighty hunter by the grace of the Lord" (Gen 10:9). He was also "the first man of might on earth" (10:8). Scholars connect this mighty hunter with the historical Tukutli-Ninurta I (ca. 1234–1197 BCE), the Assyrian monarch who conquered Babylon and was known for hunting. He was the first ruler who combined Babylon and Assyria under a single authority/government. Ninurta was the name of the Babylonian god of war and hunting. It was suggested, that he was identified with Nimrod. The mention of Nimrod in the Table of Nations indicates the existence of a well-known and widespread narrative about him. Hence, the Biblical narrator borrowed this motif of Nimrod, while the author chose not to keep him as a god, but instead made him a mighty hunter.

As Enoch and Nimrod were mythical heroes, so it is suggested that Samson was also a mythical hero. This is because mythological qualities have been recognized in the Samson story. Samson's name is from the Hebrew root s.m.s שמש "sun," his birth place was across the Valley of Sorek, a short distance from the city of Beth-Shemesh "house of sun," the site of a shrine of the sun god. Samson displays extraordinary strength. He slays a lion; ties foxes with blazing torches attached to their tails—the foxes with blazing torches were the withering blight on agricultural crops. He also pulls up the heavy city gate of Gaza and carries the gate for nearly 40 miles to the hilltop near Hebron. His hair was compared to the rays of the sun. All of these actions contributed to the comparison with sun heroes of Greek, Phoenician and Babylonian mythology such as Hercules, Melkart, and Gilgamesh. This study examines the alleged mythological elements that are found in our story. We will compare Samson to the mythological heroes of the ancient world to see if, indeed, Samson was a mythical hero.

Samson Kills a Lion

Samson, along with his parents, went down to Timnah to arrange his marriage with his bride-to-be. Arriving at the vineyards of Timnah, a young lion כפיר (*kephair*) ran roaring toward him. Radak pointed out that the lion is mentioned by different Hebrew words, which refers to the various stages of its growth starting with גור *gur*, כפיר *kephair*, אריה *aryeh*, לביא *labi*, and ליש *layish*. The word כפיר *kephair* is used in the Bible for young lion, which signifies a full-grown cub. In the Hebrew Bible, we find many stories about lions who attack and devour (1Kgs 13:24–28; 20:36). The roar of the lion is an example as well as a parable of a frightening and scary voice (Amos 3:4–8). This is also a recurring motif in the description of God who punishes the enemy (Jer 25:30; Joel 4:16; Amos 1:2).

Samson averted the lion's attack as the spirit of the Lord rested on him. He tore the lion as one who tears a kid. Samson tore the lion apart like a kid, which is the smallest domestic animal, hence, demonstrating his great strength. All of this he did with his bare hands, he had nothing else. According to Abravanel, this was indicative that Samson would contend with the Philistines alone, without the use of weapons. This description came to increase impressiveness of his strength, but the Bible tells us that this was done when the spirit of the Lord gripped him. Heroic stories that describe fighting against animals, and in particular lions, are found in the Book of Samuel, thus, David "slew the lion" (17:36) and Benaiah ben Jehoiada "slew a lion in the midst of a pit" (2Sam 23:20–21; 1Chr 11:22).

Similar stories of killing a lion are mentioned in the Greek mythology. Ademetus subdued a lion to get the hand of Alcestis.[4] Phylius tamed a lion to receive the favors of Cycnus.[5] Additionally, Pulydams of Scotusa in Thessaly, moved by desire to emulate the feats of Hercules, is said to have slain a large and powerful lion on Mount Olympus without weapons.[6] Heracles is the hero of myths and cults and is celebrated in ancient Greek literature often described as the greatest of all the Greek heroes. By the time he is 18 years old, he has attained legendary status. His first great feat is strangling a lion at Cytheiron bare-handed in order to get the favors of the 50 daughters of Thespius.[7] Comparable to our story is the story of Heracles strangling the Nemean lion: "with nothing in his hands,"[8] which compares to Judges 14:6 " ... and he had nothing in his hands." The story is the first of his 12 trials. According to the story, the people of Nemea could not kill the lion that was killing them and their livestock. This lion was twice the size of a regular lion. He first stunned the lion with a blow of his club. The lion ran into its cave, which allegedly had two openings, one of which Heracles had blocked.[9] Then he strangled it to death with his bare hands. To prove his

---

4 Hyginus, *Fabula* 50; Margalith, "Legends of Samson/Heracles," 67 no.15.

5. Ovid, *Metamorphoses* vii.371ff.

6. Pausanias, vi.5.

7. Apollodorus, II.4.10; Pausanias, IX.27.6–7; Margalith, "Legends of Samson/Heracles," 67 no.20

8. Margalith, "Legends of Samson/Heracles," 67 no.23.

9. Diodorus of Sicily, 4.11.4.

victory, Heracles is expected to bring the pelt of the lion to King Eurystheus. Heracles tries to cut the pelt but with no success. Finally he uses the claws of the creature to cut its own skin. He brings the pelt to Eurystheus, but in the end, keeps it as his own personal armor. According to one of the traditions, Zeus decided to honor his son so he transported the monster to the skies as a memorial, where it became the Lion in the Zodiac.[10]

Another mythical hero who killed a lion is Gilgamesh. According to the story, Gilgamesh is in mourning for Enkidu. After Enkidu's death, Gilgamesh became aware of his own mortality. He leaves Uruk to find the immortal Uta-napishti who has the secret of immortality. On the road one night he arrives at a mountain pass where he sees some lions. He prays to his god Sin to keep him safe. That night he wakes up and "he smote the [lions, he] killed them and scattered them."[11]

In addition to mythical heroes, there are descriptions of kings from the Ancient Near East who are depicted as hunting lions in Ancient Near Eastern iconography and literatures. The kings of the Neo-Assyrian Empire were known as lion hunters. One description tells how one of the kings boasted: "I killed 370 strong lions like caged birds with the spear."[12] The difference from our story is that they are depicted striking down the lions with weapons such as spears, bow and arrow, or sword. They hunted lions while they were riding a horse or in a chariot and sometimes on foot.[13] They used different methods to hunt lions. Killing a lion was prestigious and it added glory and stature to the king. Not surprisingly, the lion was a royal symbol and was an epithet to kings from Sumer to the Neo-Assyria. We should point out that in the Hebrew Bible the lions were compared with the tribe of Judah (Gen 49:9) and Dan (Deut 33:22). Balaam in his oracle said of the Israelites: "Lo, a people that rises like a lion, Leaps up like the king of the beasts . . ." (Num 23:24).

A question about this story needs to be asked. What was the purpose of it? Did the story come to tell the reader about the strength of Samson and his future act of strength? Or can we say that the story appeared to prepare the reader for the riddle that follows. More likely, the narrator had these two reasons in mind. Noteworthy, that the heroic actions by Samson are a prelude to his future fight with the Philistines, and interestingly, the David

---

10. Condos, *Star Myths*, 125
11. George, *Epic of Gilgamesh*, 70.
12. Grayson, *Assyrian Royal Inscription*, 2:150.no.600.
13. Cornelius, "Lion in the Art," 55–8.

story starts in a similar way. David tried to convince Saul that he was the right man to defeat Goliath. To persuade him, he mentions his past heroic actions, which included killing a lion. Hence, David like Samson, starts his heroic actions by killing a lion and afterward he continually fights against the Philistines. The phrase "and nothing in his hand" (14:6), came to emphasize Samson's strength, which distinguishes him from other people who slew lions.

Jawbone of an Ass

When Samson was brought to the Philistines' camp they shouted excitedly. This was the cry of victory at the sight of seeing Samson handcuffed. This joyous cry changes immediately when the Spirit of the Lord came upon him. The ropes that tied Samson fall from his arms and wrists. Samson is at the center of the enemy camp with no weapon. Suddenly he finds a new jawbone of an ass and with this, he smites 1,000 men. In ancient times the jawbone of an ass was used as a tool, especially as a scythe from the end of the Stone Age to the beginning of the Bronze Age. Instead of a tooth, the farmer inserted a flint knife. In addition to its agricultural use it was also used as a weapon, therefore, it is not a mere coincidence that Samson had in his hand the jawbone of an ass.[14] This is the first time that we read that Samson had a weapon in his hand, which was not mentioned in his previous attacks. The use of a jawbone of an ass is reminiscent of Shamgar's victory against the Philistines with an ox goad (3:31). The Bible mentions that it was a fresh jawbone of a donkey, which is much stronger than an old one that can disintegrate. This story is also reminiscent of David's hero, Shammah son of Age the Ararite, who slew the Philistines according to the LXX at Lehi (2Sam 23:11–12). There is a difference between the two stories, Samson fought his own private battle, while Shammah was fighting for his nation.

Some similarities to our story appear in a tale about Heracles who picks up an olive tree and turns it into a lethal weapon, according to one version, at Helicon[15] and another at Nemea[16] or at Saronic Sea.[17] This became his preferred weapon, and he was using it even to uproot a tree from which he

---

14. Marglit, "Parallel between the Samson story," 125
15. Theocritus, *Idyll* xxv.207–10.
16. Apollodorus, II.4.11
17. Pausanias, II.31.10

made an oar.[18] There are traditions from twelfth-century Europe that depict Samson as the mythical hero who is uprooting a tree.[19] This is strange since the Bible makes no mention of Samson uprooting a tree. We don't know the reason for this portrayal. The Haggadah (Jewish legends) recounts Samson tearing out two mountains and rubbing them against each other.[20] In another story in the Haggadah, in order to enlist in Bar Kochba's army, people were required to prove their strength by uprooting a cedar.[21]

Moore took a different direction, he pointed to some similarities between this story and the Islamic tradition. According to him, the first blood for the cause of Islam was drawn with a similar weapon. A group of Meccan idolaters met the believers at prayers in a remote place, words led to blows, and Sa'dibn Abī Waqqāṣ broke the head of one of the heathen with jawbone.[22]

The story of Samson killing 1,000 Philistines with the jawbone of an ass came to glorify Samson and his strength. It is true that by killing so many people his actions are similar to mythological heroes. However, the mythological heroes are gods or sons of gods. Their strength lies in their divine origin. Not so with Samson who is an earthly hero who fights with humans without the aid of any magical weapons but with the jawbone of an ass.

The Gates of Gaza

In contrast to other stories where Samson slayed many Philistines, in the story of the harlot from Gaza he not only humiliated the Philistines, he put them to shame. Indeed, in the previous chapter Samson killed 1,000 Philistines for attempting to capture him (15:15–16). Here, although the Philistines try to kill him, he does not retaliate physically against them. Instead, he carried the gate of the city to the top of the hill: "At midnight he got up, grasped the doors of the town gate together with the two gateposts, and pulled them out along with the bar. He placed them on his shoulders and carried them off to the top of the hill near Hebron" (v.3). Samson demonstrates his great physical strength here by uprooting and carrying the gates a great distance. He carried the gates to Hebron, which is 50 km

---

18. Ovid, *Metamorphoses*, IX.234
19. Scheiber, "Samson Uprooting a Tree," 176–80; and Scheiber, "Further Parallels," 35–40.
20. *b. Soṭah. 9b.*
21. *Eccles. R.* 2:8.
22. More, *Judges*, 345.

east of Gaza. The narrator emphasizes the ease of Samson's act, which is in contrast to the Philistines who conspired all night to capture him, yet failed. Hence, even if the Philistines find the gates it would be very difficult for them to return the gates to their city.

The motif of the two doors that rested on Samson's shoulders is well-known in Greek mythology. Heracles was known as the gatekeeper of the gods at Mount Olympus. According to the legend, Heracles was consecrated by Zeus on his death and was given the task as the keeper of the Gates of Mount Olympus.[23] In other words, he was supposed to hold the gates open for the gods who arrived home late, particularly the huntress Artemis. Another motif that these heroes share is embracing two pillars, where Samson is in the temple of Dagon (16:29) and Heracles is setting up his pillars. The image of Heracles with mighty pillars in each of his arms is well-known. These pillars of Heracles were identified at Gibraltar and the rock of Abyla, Abila, or Abylica on the northern and southern sides of the straits.[24]

Samson and the Foxes

Following the loss of his wife, Samson acts against the Philistines in a unusual way:

> Samson went and caught three hundred foxes. He took torches and, turning [the foxes] tail to tail, he placed a torch between each pair of tails. He lit the torches and turned [the foxes] loose among the standing grain of the Philistines, setting fire to stacked grain, standing grain, vineyards, [and] olive trees (Judg 15:4–5).

Scholars claim that foxes are self-contained animals and it would be impossible to tie them together.[25] More so, they are rare in the Land of Israel. Therefore, it was suggested that it was jackals not foxes that also live in packs and are much easier to capture. It is more likely that Samson indeed captured 300 foxes, yet the Bible wanted to stress the unique power of Samson because he acted in a way that regular people cannot emulate. Interestingly, in contrast to his first encounter with the lion where the spirit of Yahweh rushed into him, now there is no mention of divine intervention.

23. Margalith, "Legends of Samson," 69.
24. The opinions of the ancient were divided on the subject of the location of the pillars of Hercules see: Ibid., 70. no.29.
25. Soggin, *Judges*, 246.

Mythical Elements in the Samson Story

Nevertheless, there is a sense that there is a guiding hand behind Samson. It is God who is behind Samson's acts. It's noteworthy that this is the second time we find Samson's actions associated with animals. The first time Samson killed the lion; now he uses the foxes in his battle against the Philistines. Later he will use the jawbone of a donkey to strike down 1,000 men (v.15).

Scholars point to Ovid's writings, which mention the foxes with blazing torches attached to their tails that were let loose in the Hippodrome. This type of event took place annually at the Circus in Rome during the Cerealia, April 19. It is believed that this was a ritual to protect the crops. In other words, it was a symbolic act as a form of lustration by fire where mildew and other harmful elements were consumed. Later Ovid explains this custom, which is a tale he had heard from an old countryman of Carseoli. According to the tale, a farmer's son who was 12 years old caught a vixen fox that robbed his father's hen-roosts, wrapped it in straw and hay, then proceeded to set it on fire. The fox escaped and rushed through the fields of corn and set them on fire. Therefore, a law was set in Carseoli that dealt with the fate of captured foxes.

Evidently, this story has nothing to do with the festival of the Cerealia. The significance of this rite was lost. Scholars suggest this refers to a public rite, which came to avert blight and mildew by using heat made by live animals. Similarly, among the Arabs during a drought, cattle with lighted torches tied to their tails were sent to the mountains so they would bring down rainfall and fertility.[26] Literary sources from Mesopotamia reveal there were many rituals whose purpose was to protect the crops in the fields. Indeed, the Sumerian Georgics implore farmers to practice proper rites for the different stages of the growth of grain.[27] Among the rituals mentioned is the burning of plants in or near fields in order to protect them.

However, these explanations have no bearing on our story. Samson set fire to destroy the Philistine's fields not to protect them. By setting fire to the Philistine's fields, the narrator foreshadows Samson's future fight with the Philistine god Dagon who was the god of grain. The god Dagon is the only Philistine god who is mentioned in our story. Direct confrontation between the God of Israel and Dagon ends the Samson stories. Our hero will topple the temple of Dagon with all the people in it.

The use of foxes by Samson exemplifies a clever military tactic. This can be compared to Hannibal who fooled the Roman troops at Lake

---

26. Wellhausen, *Reste arabischen Heidentums*, 167
27. Civil, *Farmer's Instructions*, 177.

Trasimene in 217 BCE by sending into their fields oxen with firebrands tied to their horns.[28] Similarly, the Mongols who attacked the Arabs near Aleppo sent foxes and hounds with torches attached to their tails. In the Hebrew Bible, the Gideon story describes torches carried by men in order to cause mayhem in the enemy camp (Judg 7:16–19). It is possible that Samson used foxes because they equate to destruction. In the Book of Song of Songs we read: "Catch us the foxes, the little foxes that ruin the vineyards For our vineyard is in blossom" (2:15). Just like in this story, the foxes are mentioned with the destruction of vineyards. Similarly, in Sumerian text, the fox is equated with doom and compared to demons that enter the town at night dragging their tails on the ground.[29]

Solar Myth

In ancient times, acts of power were originally attributed to the Sun; it was "the conqueror of gloomy night." Later, the sun motif was transferred to a local hero. The name Samson is derived from the Hebrew שמש *shemesh*, which means sun, so it was suggested that Samson's narrative is a solar myth. The man of God who came to Samson's parents is described: "As the flames leaped up from the altar toward the sky, the angel of the Lord ascended in the flames of the altar" (Judg 13:20). This is a typical description of a sun god who ascends from the east in flames of fire toward the sky. It suits our narrative because we later read that his mother named him Samson, which means "sun man." Similarly, we read about Hercules, who by the end of his life ascends in fire to Olympus to his father Zeus. Samson operated near a place named Beth-Shemesh, "Temple of the Sun", which indicates that people in that vicinity worshipped the sun. Samson was from the tribe of Dan. According to Burney, the tribe of Dan referred originally to a divine Judge who was the patron of the tribe. In Babylon the chief Judge was Šamaš the Sun-god whose title among the Babylonians and Assyrians was Dân.[30] Samson is described as fighting against various animals: hence, Samson the hero, symbolized by the sun fights the animals in the heavenly Zodiac as the sun moves in its yearly cycle.

The name Samson is probably connected to the worship of sun but this does not prove that Samson himself worshipped the sun. On the

28. Gaster, *Myth, Legend, and Custom*, 435.
29. Guillaume, *Waiting for Josiah*, 178.
30. Burney, *Judges*, 392.

contrary, throughout the story the narrator stresses the fact that Samson receives his power from God. Sun worship is mentioned in the Hebrew Bible in later periods (see below), so if this was the case, it is not clear why the author does not mention it here or condemn it. The description of the angel ascending in flames has nothing to do with a sun god who ascends in flames toward the sky. Elijah also ascended to God in chariots of fire. In the Hebrew Bible, fire is the consistent element of the description of theophany.

Sculptures, paintings, and literature of ancient times portray the long, magnificent rays that come from the sun, as the locks of hair that are found on the head of a hero.[31] This comparison of the sun's rays and Samson's hair is superficial. Samson's hair has nothing to do with the sun's rays. The sun's rays are its power, they are warming the earth and burning. Not so with Samson's hair, this is the secret of his power, not his weapon. When the sun goes down it gathers its rays, "it is dying." Samson, on the other hand, dies when his hair starts to grow. We can see that there is no compelling reason to compare Samson's hair with the sun's rays.

Another attempt to display the solar traits in the Samson story is by comparing him to Gilgamesh, the Babylonian mythical hero who shares similar adventures and characteristics to Samson. It is believed that Gilgamesh is a solar hero. He is not identical with Šamaš, but he is under his protection. As the sun passes through heaven so does Gilgamesh, following the sun's path, he goes where no one but the sun has been.[32] Gilgamesh undergoes changes as the sun goes through its yearly course. There are some incidents where Gilgamesh and the Sun god are used interchangeably. For example, they are described as killing the same animals.

As noted above, the sun's rays are compared to hair in the literature of many nations throughout time. The sun's rays have great strength in the summer but are weaker in the winter. Similar traits are found with Gilgamesh, when in the springtime he appears as the glorious sun; where it is said that he wears his long hair falling down his back. The text does not mention that Gilgamesh loses his long locks when he becomes ill but loses his strength. However, Burney suggests that since they are mentioned when he was young and strong and not mentioned when he is weak, he probably lacked long locks.[33] Samson's strength is in his hair, but he loses that strength when he shaves it. To reiterate, Samson's hair has nothing to do

---

31. Palmer, *Samson–Saga*, 34.
32. Burney, *Judges*, 396.
33. Ibid., 404.

with the sun's rays. It is not clear if Gilgamesh, indeed, was a solar hero. More so, as Burney admitted, it is very difficult to distinguish solar traits in the Samson narrative and "the interpretation as a solar trait must remain extremely precarious."[34]

Solar mythology pointed to the bursting forth of spring at Ramath-leḥi. The hot springs were associated with the sun or solar heroes. It is believed that the springs are warmed by the sun. According to Athenaeus (xii. 512), all hot springs that break from the earth are sacred to Heracles. The hot springs burst from the earth so the solar hero can bathe in them when weary. Bathing in the warm spring as Heracles does or drinking from the cool spring as Samson did, according to Burney, have the same effect the hero regains his vitality.[35] Similarly, the sun regains its power in spring. As Gilgamesh bathes to regain his strength and free himself from diseases, so the sun regains its strength after the winter. However, as we mentioned before, the aim of Samson's story is to diminish the image of Samson as a [an unstoppable] mighty hero who could overcome every obstacle. Instead, the narrator inserts a religious flavor by stating it was not Samson's own power behind his victory, but it was God's power. More so, the descriptions of God bringing out water for the thirsty is a repeated motif in the Hebrew Bible. The most notable story is about Moses who struck the rock in order to get water.

Scholars have observed connections between Samson and the Zodiac solar god Leo. Samson found honey in the carcass of the lion, which he had killed in the past. The sun produces sweet honey when it is in the constellation of Leo. Honey is a gift of the solar god. The Greek Aristaeus who invented honey is identified with a solar god. He is the protector of bees and their hives, he delivered the Island of Kios from a lion.[36] Honey is not the only gift of the sun; every other food is also a gift from the sun. Samson is not inventing honey or bees, instead, he only finds the honey, therefore, he is not like the Greek Aristaeus. Samson finding honey in the carcass of a lion has nothing to do with a solar god. His story resembles the story of Jonathan who also found honey (1Sam 14:27).

---

34. Ibid., 403.
35. Ibid.,406.
36 Palmer, *Samson-Saga*, 99.

Sun Worship

Veneration for celestial bodies can be traced back to the second millennium BCE in Syria –Palestine. In the Hebrew Bible, as mentioned before, sun worship is forbidden (Deut 4:19; 17:3), and Job denied doing so: "If I ever saw the light shining, the moon on its course in full glory, and I was secretly lured and my hand touched my mouth in kiss . . ." (Job 31:26–27). This passage articulates the seductiveness of idolatry of the heavenly bodies. The worship of the sun and the moon was common in the Ancient Near East. However, in the Hebrew Bible the heavenly bodies are God's servants; they are subordinate to the Lord and dependent on Him (Ps 74:16). It is noteworthy that the sun is a real deity given to the other nations by Yahweh (Deut 4:19). In light of the importance of the sun cult in the Ancient Near East, it is strange that it is rarely mentioned in the Hebrew Bible. Scriptures from the time of Joshua and the Book of Judges do not mention it. Only the Book of Kings mentions sun worship when it speaks of the sins of Northern Israel (2Kgs 17:16). Nevertheless, it does not attribute the sins to the kings themselves. Thus, it was [probably] a popular cult, albeit an unofficial one. In Judea the sun cult is mentioned with King Manasseh who built altars to the sun in the temple (2Kgs 21:5). Josiah removed horses dedicated to the sun from the temple entrance and burned "the chariots of the sun" (2Kgs 23:11). Most likely this form of cult began in Israel as a result of the Assyrian influence during the reign of Ahaz and reached its peak during the time of Manasseh. Indeed, Manasseh is blamed for building altars for the entire host of heavenly bodies (2Kgs 21:5). White horses appear in ritual functions in Assyria and were associated with the gods Ashur and Sin. Shamash, the sun god, rode a horse-drawn chariot as well as the other Mesopotamian deities. Hence, the mention of horses in the 2Kings 23:11 suggests that similar rites existed in Judah.[37] Josiah's attempt to uproot this form of cult did not succeed; and before the Babylonian exile, the prophet Ezekiel describes priests worshipping the sun in the courtyard of the temple in Jerusalem (Ezek 8:16). We can see that Sun worship developed in the later periods, since there is not a single mention of it in the Books of Joshua and Judges. This leads us to the conclusion that Samson did not worship the sun and the connection between Samson and the solar myth is purely imaginative. More so if this was the case, it is not clear why the author did not mention it here or, alternatively, condemn it.

---

37. Cogan and Tadmor, *II Kings*, 288.

Conclusion

In conclusion, Samson's deeds are somewhat similar to other mythological heroes. Like other mythological heroes he is powerful and his strength is superhuman. But there is a major difference between Samson and the mythological heroes. The mythological heroes are the gods or sons of gods. Their strength lays in their divine origin. They are fighting against gods and sons of gods, demons and dragons.[38] Not so for Samson, who is a human fighting against the Philistines who are real people. The Hebrews did not live in a vacuum; they were familiar with mythical legends of other cultures. Their monotheistic religion had to cope with it. Hence, what they did was to demythologize those stories and strip them of their mythological elements and use them to show the superiority of their God. Hence, Shemesh and Dagon are both supplanted by Yahweh. Four times in the Samson story, the narrator declares that "the Spirit of the Lord" moved Samson (Judg 13: 25; 14:6, 9; 15:14). It is the spirit of God that gives Samson his power to slay the lion bare-handed, to kill 30 people at Ashkelon, to break the rope the men of Judah tied him with, and to kill 1,000 men with a jawbone. Indeed, after his victory at Lehi, Samson acknowledged that it was God who was responsible for his triumph. More so, before his final act, Samson prayed to God to give him strength and God answered his prayer. Everything that he did is local and personal. Finally, as Simon points out: "The Samson story has indeed earthiness. . .which removes it from mythology."[39]

Now that we know Samson's strength is from God, we need to find out more about the Philistines. These people take up much of the Samson story narrative. We'll explore their place of origin, where they came from, as well as their culture and customs.

---

38. Kaufman, *Judges*, 244.
39. Simon, "Samson and the Heroic," 158.

7

Philistines

THE ISRAELITES DREADED THE Philistine confederacy, which lasted until 1000 BCE The Bible describes numerous fights between Samson and the Philistines. Later, during the time of King Saul, these fights would intensify, where, ultimately, Saul would die in his last battle against the Philistines on Mount Gilboa. Only when David became the King of Israel did the Israelites succeed in defeating the Philistines. So who were these Philistines that the Israelites were so fearful of? This chapter will examine the origin of the Philistines and where they lived. Was there any connection between the Philistines and the tribe of Dan? It has been suggested: to identify the tribe of Dan with the Danaans of Homer and Denyen as mentioned in Ramesses III's inscription. In order to understand the Philistines and see who these people were, we will examine their culture. This will include their political organizations, military, livelihood, language and religion.

The People and Their Origin

The Philistines are mentioned in Egyptian text as *prst* which is one of the names of the "People of the sea." They invaded Egypt in the eighth year of Ramses III (ca.1190 BCE). The name appears also in Assyrian sources as *Pilišti* and *Palaštu/Palastu* (also *Palaštaya*). The LXX when not translating it as "strangers" (*allopsyloi*) renders it as *phylistim* (i.e. in Genesis/Joshua).The historian Herodotus refers to them as *palastinoi* and their country *palastium*. In his works Josephus uses the terms *Philistines* and *Philistia* and calls the entire land Palestine. The name received acceptance as the Roman emperor

Hadrian called the providence of Judea *Province Palaestine* by the fourth century, hence, the short name Palaestine became the prevalent name.

The first mention of the Philistines in the Hebrew Bible appears in the "Table of Nations" in Genesis 10:14: "the Pathrusim, the Casluhim, and the Caphtorim, whence the Philistines came forth." This corresponds to *kaptaru* in Akkadian texts, and *kptr* in Ugaritic, and probably also *keftiu* in Egyptian, all of which relate to the biblical Capthorim that is identified with the isle of Crete. In Deuteronomy 2:23, we read of the Capthorim who came from Caphtor and settled in Gaza. This place became a major Philistine city during the judges' period. The prophets, Amos 9:7 and Jeremiah 47:4, mention the fact that the Philistines came from Caphtor. In two passages, the Cretans appear in parallelism with the Philistines (Ezek 25: 16; Zeph 2:5). In Ezekiel we read: "Behold, I will stretch out my hand against the Philistines, and I will cut off the Cherethites, and destroy the rest of the sea-coast." Additionally, in Zephaniah: "For Gaza shall be deserted, and Ashkelon shall become a desolation; Ashadod's people shall be driven out at noon, and Ekron shall be uprooted. Woe unto you, inhabitants of the sea coast, your nation of the Cherethites" (2:4). More so, part of the land where the Philistines dwelled was called "the Cretan Negeb" (1Sam 30:14). This area was controlled by the Philistines and probably was in the vicinity of Ziklag. Later we read of the presence of Cherethites in David's and Solomon's army. This loyalty to the house of David has its roots from the period of time David spent at Ziklag.

The Philistines probably came over land through Anatolia destroying the Hittite empire, Ugarit, and Amurru; and by ship via Crete and Cyprus (Num 24:24). Excavations in Antaolia and Syria reveal that many cities were destroyed at the end of the Late Bronze Age (ca. 1200). They were allied with other Sea People and they tried to settle in Egypt. However, their attempts failed and they suffered a major defeat by Ramesses III who clashed with them about 1190 BCE. As a result of this, Rameses settled the Philistines as Egyptian mercenaries in the coastal towns of Gaza, Ashkelon, and Ahdod. Among the "Sea People," only the Philistines who lived along the Palestinian coast and the Tjeker who settled at Dor (according to the Wen Amon story ca. 1050) can be positively identified.[1] Other people such as: Shekelesh, Denyen, Sherden, and Weshesh have only been conjecturally identified. These people probably migrated from their homeland as part of

---

1. Greenfield "Philistines," In *IDB* 3:791–92; Greenfield and Sperling, "Philistines," 16:52.

a population movement that took place at the latter half of the second millennium BCE. Findings of the Philistine's ceramics shows that they indeed arrived from Crete.

According to the biblical tradition, the Land of the Philistines is part of the coastal plain that is situated between Tel Qasile and Wadi Gahazza, which is about six miles south of Gaza. This territory extends over 1,000 square kilometers. It controls a stretch of the "Way of the Sea," which was a vital route dominated by the Canaanites and their Egyptian overlords. The Philistines Pentapolis was a confederation of five major cities: Gaza, Ashkelon, Ashdod, Gath, and Ekron. Three of these cities—Gaza, Ashkelon, and Ashdod—were on the coast. Gath was located in Western Shephelah, while Ekron was six miles inland. Each of these cities was a city state that was ruled by *seranîm*.

Philistines and the Tribe of Dan

The Book of Judges describes the clashes between the Philistines and Samson who was from the tribe of Dan. Samson is described as moving freely between the Israelites and the Philistine territories. Interestingly, in the Testament of Jacob when he addresses his sons, Jacob refers to Dan "like one of the tribes of Israel," which is puzzling. This led to some speculation as to the origin of the tribe. Gordon and Yadin suggested that the tribe of Dan joined the other tribes after the formation of the tribal confederation.[2] According to Yadin, the tribe of Dan had close relations with the Sea People. The Dan tribe was an ancient tribe that did not have any connections with the confederacy of tribes. Through the years, the tribe got closer to the tribes of Israel until it became one of them. Its place of habitat was along the coast near Jaffa. It was suggested to identify the tribe of Dan with the Danaans of Homer and Denyen as mentioned in Ramesses III's inscription. According to Yadin, this tribe's members were seafarers worshipping the sun where they lived by the eastern Mediterranean coast in the Jaffa area.[3] In the *Song of Deborah*, Dan is described as staying with ships. This is puzzling since the tribe did not have direct access to the sea coast (Judg 1:34; ch.18). Thus, it is possible that they were involved with ships through some kind of connection with the Phoenicians as hired workers. The similarities between the two groups led Yadin to the identification of the two. However,

---

2. Gordon, "Mediterranean Factor," 21–2; Yadin, "And Dan," 9–23.
3. Yadin, "And Dan," 21–2.

the similarities between the two groups can be explained as an outcome of contact and influence.

Reading the Hebrew Bible reveals that the tribe of Dan was pressed by the Amorites on the west (Judg 1:34); possibly by the house of Joseph on the east (1:35); and possibly it was pressured by Judah as well (15:11). In addition, the Philistines expanded into the Jaffa region, which is manifested by the findings of the Philistine Tell Qasile. As a result, the tribe moved northward to conquer Laish and settle there under the name Dan. According to Judges 18:27, the Danites destroyed the city of Laish and rebuilt the city and named it Dan. Archeological excavations at Tel Dan clearly point to destruction of the site. Over the ruins of a prosperous city from the Late Bronze age, a poor rural settlement was discovered. Among the findings were storage pits and a variety of collared-rim jars, but no Philistine pottery. This according to Stager shows, with no doubt, that the Danites belonged to the Israelites and not to the confederation of Sea People.[4] Samson, the Biblical hero who fought bravely against the Philistines, belonged to the tribe of Dan and lived in the original territory. de Vaux suggested that Dan was originally part of the tribe of Benjamin.[5] After the tribe of Dan moved north, the tribe was separated from the tribe of Benjamin and became autonomous. This might explain the phrase that Dan judged his people "as any other of the tribes of Israel."

The First Clashes with the Philistines

The battles between the Israelites and the Philistines are first mentioned in the Book of Judges. It describes an isolated incident of a battle between Shamgar, son of Anath, and the Philistines (Judg 3:31). Accordingly, he struck 600 Philistines with an ox goad. Shamgar operates as an individual hero similar to Samson. Later in the Book of Judges, Samson's heroic fights against the Philistines are described. This reflects a situation in which the Philistines ruled over Israel (1070 BCE). Indeed, the Bible mentions Judean fear of offending the Philistines (Judg 14:11–12), which points to the Philistines' domination. This continued pressure by the Philistines forced part of the tribe of Dan to migrate to the north to find a safer place. The Philistine expansion to the north-central town of Ephraim transpired slowly. The Israelites suffered a major defeat at Ebenezer (ca.1050 BCE), where the

4. Stager, "Forging an Identity," 167
5. de Vaux, *Early History*, 775–83.

Ark of the Covenant was captured by the Philistines. More so, the holy site of Shiloh was destroyed wiping out the Elide dynasty of priests (1Sam 4: 1–7; Jer 7:12, 14). Although Samuel temporarily gained a victory against the Philistines at Mizpah recapturing the territory "from Ekron even unto Gath" (1Sam 7:14), the people of Israel demanded a king that would lead them to a victory against the Philistines. It was during Samuel's period that the Philistines reached the height of their power. They had military bases in the hill country at Bethlehem, Geba, and Gibeath-elohim and fought the Israelites at Michmash, which is located near Jerusalem (1Sam 10:5; 13:3, 11; 2Sam 23:13–14). The King that was chosen to lead the Israelites against the Philistines was none other than Saul from the tribe of Benjamin. From the start of his reign until his tragic death on Mount Gilboa, the Book of Samuel describes Saul's battles with the Philistines. In these clashes (1Sam 14, 17, 18:27, 30, 19:8, 23:1–5, 24:1), no side achieved a total victory. This changed with Saul's last battle against the Philistines at Mount Gilboa. Following this battle, the Philistines gained control over the north-central part of Israel and the territory west of the Jordan river (1Sam 29:1, 30–31; 31:7). Israel's independence was limited to their southeastern margins, where David set his capital at Hebron, and Ishboseth, Saul's son, at Mahanaim over in the Gilead (2Sam 2:8–9)

The Philistines During the Reign of David and Salomon

When David became the King of Israel he succeeded in defeating the Philistines. The Bible describes two battles that took place in the Valley of Rephaim, where David defeated them (2 Sam 5:17–24; 1Chr 14:8–17). More so, he routed the Philistines from Geba all the way to Gezer (2Sam 5:25). From this point, David continued his battles with the Philistines until he completely destroyed them. The Bible does not describe David's wars in chronological order. In 2Sam 8:1, we read that he defeated the Philistines and seized Metheg-Amma, while in the parallel verse in 1Chr 18:11, he seized Gath and its dependencies. Other wars with the Philistines are mentioned in the heroic stories of David's warriors (2Sam 21:18–22; 23:9–17; 1 Chr 11:12–19). Living among the Philistines when Saul was trying to kill him, David learned their military tactics, which helped him defeat them. In addition, some of the mercenaries who served in his army included the Sea People. Hence, we read of Ittai the Gittite (2Sam 15:18–22) and his bodyguard the Cherethites and the Pelethites (2Sam 8:18; 15:18; 20:7, 23;

1Kgs 1:38, 44; 1Chr 18:17). In other words, for the first time the Philistines had to face a formidable force that included professional soldiers. This crushing blow by David signals the end of the Philistines Pentapolis. It is believed that after that, each city state acted independently. There are only two rulers with Philistine names that are mentioned after the battles with Saul and David: Achish of Gath (1Kgs 2:39–40), the person whom David served, and Ikausu of Ekron, a contemporary of Ashurbanipal. The rest of the Philistine rulers have Semitic names. Therefore, it is suggested that during the battles against Saul and David, the class of military rulers was wiped out and the process of assimilation and integration with the Canaanite population started. This might explain the fact that the Philistine pottery of the Early Iron Age disappeared. Instead pottery and artifacts that were found are from the Early Iron Age III levels; which are identical with what is found in the rest of the country.

Following the death of King David, his son Solomon became the king of Israel. He entered into a marriage alliance with the Pharaoh of Egypt. There is no mention of Solomon fighting against the Philistines. However, in 970/960 BCE, the Egyptians mount a campaign in which they subdued Philistia. According to 1 Kings 9, the Egyptian army captured Gezer, a Canaanite vassal city of the Philistines. The Pharaoh who mounted the campaign is identified with Siamun, of the twenty-first dynasty, who gave Gezer as a dowry to his daughter when she married Solomon.[6] According to Malamat, the Egyptian purpose for the campaign was to re-establish the hegemony over the southwestern corner of Canaan.[7] The death of a strong king like David was an opportunity for the Egyptians.[8] This alliance between Israel and Egypt benefited the two states politically and commercially. At the same time, the Phoenician commerce was expanding, hence, from the tenth century we witness the decline of the Philistines in maritime trade and control of land routes.[9]

---

6. Kitchen, "Philistines," 65.

7. Malamat, *Das davidische und salomonische Königreich*, 21, 25.

8. For different views on the Egyptians involvement in the war see: Ehrlich, *The Philistines in Transition*, 52 no144.

9. Kitchen, "Philistines," 65.

PHILISTINES

The Culture of the Philistines

Their Organization

Four of the Philistines' cities have been identified as Gaza, Ashkelon, Ashdod, and Ekron. The location of the fifth city, Gath, remains an open question. In addition to the Pentapolis, two other cities are mentioned in the Hebrew Bible, Ziklag and Timmna (1Sam. 27:5). A third city, Jabneh, is mentioned under Philistine rule during the time of Uzziah (2Chr. 26). These cities were smaller and under the control of the capital state. The Philistines' expansion into Israelite territory merited some strategic sites be fortified.

The Israelites feared the Philistine Pentapolis, which lasted until 1,000 BCE. The Philistines were ruled by the *seranim*. At the head of each city state stood a *seran*. The word is probably a cognate of the Greek word *tyrannos* (English "tyrant"). Interestingly, the Philistine leader is sometimes referred to as a king, hence, we read of Achish the king of Gath (1Sam 21:11; 27:2). Nevertheless, the Philistines were not ruled by one person. This is recorded in their meeting at Ashdod when they captured the Ark and brought it to their city. The men of Ashdod and Ekron are summoned by the lords for advice on how to react to the outbreak of the plague. We also read of disagreements between the Philistine commanders *(seranim)* and Achish questioning David's joining them in the battle against Saul at Gilboa (1Sam 29:4–10). It appears that during the time of crisis they would meet and decide together what action to take. According to Dothan, it is not clear whether the office of *seran* was hereditary or elected.[10] Examination of Assyrian sources that relate to the Philistines shows that it was hereditary. We find the chain of rulers over Ashdod included fathers and sons, but the ruler could be deposed by the population. It is believed that the social organization of the Philistines was based on military aristocracy. Thus, their military organization, their tactics, and weaponry allow them to control the land of Israel for a long period.

Military

The *seranim* who ruled the Philistines also served as commanders of the army. The military forces of the Philistines were well organized. The army

---

10. Dothan, *Philistines*, 19.

was composed of infantry, archers (1Sam 13), chariotry, and horseman (1Sam 13). According to 1Samuel 13:5, the Philistines had 30,000 chariots and 6,000 horseman, which points to a structured army. The infantry was divided into groups of hundreds and thousands (1Sam 29:2). Judges 1:19 mentions their use of war chariots, while in the description of the battle of Gilboa, archers are mentioned. In the battle of Michmas, they launched their attacks from garrisons, which were located at strategic points (1Sam 14:15). The Philistine force that launched its attacks is referred to as the "raiding party." It appears that in order to maintain their control of the Israelite territory, they would send those forces occasionally to repel a rebellion.

A different form of battle that was known to the Philistines, while alien to the Israelites, was the battle at the valley of Elah between David and Goliath. It presents us with a different type of warfare in addition to giving us a description of the Philistine armaments. This was a battle between two people and not a battle between armies, with each side sending his champion. This single battle would determine the outcome of the war, making the losers the slaves of the victors. There are many examples from the Ancient Near East and classical sources that describe a battle between two representatives. The Iliad records the battle between Paris and Menelaus, as well as the famous encounter between Hector and Achilles. From the Ancient Near East we read of Sinuhe the Egyptian with the mighty man of Retenu.

The description of Goliath's armor is our main source for the Philistine weaponry from this biblical account. He wore a helmet and he was dressed in scaled or plated cuirass, which was believed to weigh 126 pounds. He had bronze greaves on his legs, and a bronze scimitar between his shoulders. The shaft of his spear is compared to a weaver's beam. Yadin renders this a javelin and says that a weaver's beam refers to the shape and nature of Goliath's javelin not to its size.[11] The iron spear weighed 15 or 16 pounds. A shield-bearer preceded him. This is similar to weapons used by the Homeric heroes in the Iliad and Odyssey.[12] The use of bronze, however, was likely already archaic, since by that time the Philistines' weapons were iron. Indeed, this description does not match the portrayal of Philistine warriors in the Egyptian sources. Nevertheless, it shows how well he was prepared and armed, indeed a frightening vision.

---

11. Yadin, "Goliath's Javelin," 58–9.
12. *Il.* 6.318; 7.41; *Od.*18.378.

Livelihood

Their environment provided them with the ability to become a maritime as well as an agrarian power. The Philistines took advantage of their location. Their cities Ashdod, Ashkelon, and Gaza are built on the coast. Hence, their accesses to the sea gave them opportunities for fishing and shipping. In the tale of Wen-Amon from the eleventh century, we read that Philistines, other Sea People, and the Phoenicians controlled the commerce on the sea. They exported grain, wine, and oil to neighboring countries. Their territory was suitable for the cultivation of grapes. A royal winery with a pressing room was found at Ashkelon as well as near Ashdod. More so, large vases with two handles known as kraters were found, which were used in Ancient Greece for diluting wine. It is customarily found in the dining room on a tripod. Kraters were popular among the Mycenaeans, then the Philistines evidently continued to mix wine with water. The Philistines used large bell-shaped vessels for serving wine and small bell shaped cups for drinking it. This vase had a built-in filter that strained out the debris as the liquid was drained.

The inner coastal region with its fertile land was ideal for growing wheat and olives. Not surprisingly, oil was one of the main commodities of the Philistines' exports. They traded oil with the Levant and Egypt. By the seventh-century BCE, Ekron had become the oil capital of the country. More than 100 oil facilities were found within the city. Since the Egyptians could not grow olives, the Philistines accommodated this demand. The Philistines also grew wheat, and interestingly, they made the Canaanite god Dagon their deity.

Like the Israelites and the Canaanites, the Philistines also raised sheep and goats. However, in contrast to their neighbors, they also raised pigs. Indeed, bones of pigs were found in large numbers in their place of habitat. It became the determining factor whether or not the site was of the Israelites, Canaanites, or Philistines. Pork meat was an important ingredient in the Greek diet, and it appears that the Philistines brought from home their culinary taste.

The Philistines not only controlled the maritime trade but the land trade as well. The major trade routes that connect Mesopotamia to Egypt, called the coastal highway, went through their territory. Hence, they controlled the sea and land trade in southern Levant. Not surprisingly, their cities were cosmopolitan, and many items from all over the Mediterranean were found in their cities.

The Samson Story

The Philistines were aware of ecology. Signs of urban planning are evident in their cities because they were clever urban planners. The Israelites, on the other hand, were mostly shepherds and farmers who were less sophisticated and living in the hills. Excavation at Ekron (Tel Miqne) reveals that it was a well-planned fortified city, which included industrial and elite quarters. Their homes were made of mud bricks having several rooms. At the center of the city were public buildings including a palace with shrines. The palace was part of a larger complex that included rooms with altars and a number of bronze and iron artifacts that had cultic significance. These rooms opened to a hall in which was constructed a circular hearth flanked by two-pillars bases.[13] An important element in the palaces of the Aegean world was the hearth but not so in Canaan. This architectural element embodied a tradition that reflected the social structure and habits of everyday life for the Aegean people.

In the city of Tell Qasile, located on the north bank of the Yarkon River, there were three superimposed temples discovered dating from the end of the twelfth century to the beginning of the tenth-century BCE, which were in addition to the industrial and residential structures. These structures included mud brick platforms, mud brick benches, pillars, and small chambers at the back of the temple.

Additional signs that the Philistines existed comes from pottery. From the first half of the twelfth century, pottery attributed to the Philistines was found in the places of habitat in their cities as well as in areas in the mountain regions and valleys. This was not imported pottery, because studies show that it was made with local clays. The vessels that were found recall Late Mycenaean pottery and relate to pottery from Sinda in northeast Cyprus and from Perati in Atica. The Philistines' pottery had distinctive features, which included a wide range of motifs painted in black and red; among them were colorful fish designs. Also common among them were paintings of birds preening themselves with one wing raised and the head turned back. Large vases with two handles or kraters used in Ancient Greece to mix wine and water were also found. This in addition to single-handled beer jugs with strainer spouts.

As for family life among the Philistines, not much is known. We already mentioned Samson's marriage with the Timnite. The wife remains in her father's house and Samson visited her from time to time. This type of marriage is known as *tsadiqah*. It appears that men and women were

---

13. Dothan, "Philistines," In *ABD* 5:330.

mingling as we read of the Philistines' celebrations at the temple of Dagon in Gaza.

Language

No written documents were found that might refer to the Philistines' language. It appears the Israelites and the Philistines were communicating freely. The Philistines probably were using a Canaanite dialect. One of the clues to the Philistines' language is the Hebrew Bible; examination shows that there are several words that point to the Philistine origin. The word *seren* (plural *serānîm* "lords") is a word that the Israelites acquired as a loan word. This word refers to the leaders of the Philistine confederacy. It is probably of Indo-European origin deriving from the Anatolian/Aegan sphere, and it is associated with the Hittite title *kuriwana* (*tarwana*) or with the Gk. *týrannos*.[14] There are two names that have the Philistine origin, one of them is Goliath, which is not Semitic but "Philistine," perhaps Anatolian. It appears only in 1 Samuel 17:4; in the rest of the narrative David's adversary is called the "Philistine." The second name is Achish, which is also of Philistine origin. According to Mitchell, it "is found in a list of what are described as kftiw [Cretan] names on an Egyptian school writing–board probably of the Eighteenth Dynasty, and is probably cognate with Anchises, the name, according to Homer, of a Trojan, the father of Aeneas."[15] Noteworthy is that a seventh-century temple inscription of Achish the ruler of Ekron was found. It is written in a Canaanite dialect and the spelling of Achish in the inscription is identical with the biblical spelling. In the Book of Genesis 26:1, Abimelech is the name of the king of the Philistines. The meaning of the name is "the [Divine] Father is King" or "the [Divine] King is father." The name is an ancient Semitic name attested in the form Abi-milki as the name of the King of Tyre in the fourteenth-century BCE. Scholars believed that the Philistines did not dwell in the area until 1200 BCE. Van Seters claims that this is proof of the lack of historicity in the Genesis narrative.[16] Wiseman, on the other hand, points to the area of Grear as part of an earlier migration of the Philistines.[17] From the later period, names such as Ahimilki, Sidqa, Mitinti, and Hanun are believed

---

14. Schunck "סרן srn," In *TDOT* 10:351.
15. Mitchell, "Philistia," 415.
16. Van Seters, *Abraham in History*, 52.
17. Wiseman, "Abraham Reassessed," 150.

to be Canaanite. It is suggested that the Philistines, upon their arrival to the land of Palestine, adopted a Canaanite dialect, which later gave away to Aramaic. Another clue to the Philistine language and writings are the stamp seals that were found from the twelfth century at Ashdod. These seals were used to imprint a lump of clay affixed to a letter. The text is apparently related to Linear A and B scripts and the Cypro-Minoan syllabary used in the Aegean during LB age.

Religion

In the Aegean culture, female deities were worshipped. Not so with the Philistines who replaced their gods with male gods from the Canaanite Pantheon. The head of the Philistines' Pantheon was Dagon to whom temples were dedicated in Gaza and Ashdod (Judg 16:23; 1Sam 5:1–7), and possibly also at Beth-shan (1Chr 10:10). Dagon was the chief god of Ebla (third millennium BCE) and the Lord of Terqa and other cities in the Middle of the Euphrates in the old Babylonian period. The name is probably of West Semitic origin. Different interpretations were given to the name. The Medieval Jewish commentators, such as Rashi and Radak, connected it with the Northwest Semitic word for "fish," hence, it means "the one of the fish, the fish god." Another interpretation equates it with a Semitic root *dgn*, which refers to cloud and rain. In other words, Dagon is a god of fertility. Indeed, Dagon is viewed as the father of the great storm Ba'l Haddu. Most likely the term for grain (in Hebrew *dāgān*) is derived from his name. Text from Emar, for example, mentions Dagon as "lord of the seeds" and "lord of military camp."[18] When the Philistines adopted Dagon as their own deity is not clear, but according to the Hebrew Bible, he was the national god of Philistia (1Chr 10:10). Hence, it is possible that he was adopted as a corn god by the Philistines. The temples of Gaza and Ashdod and possibly at Beth-shan were dedicated to him. A statue of Dagon made of clay stood in the temple at Ashdod (1Sam 5:2–4).[19]

Another god, Baal-Zebub has its temple in Ekron. The name Baal Zebub occurs only four times in the Hebrew Bible (2Kgs 1:2, 3, 6, 16). In 2Kings, the king of Israel Ahaziah fell through the lattice in his upper chamber, and he sent messengers to consult the oracle of the god Baal Zebub of Ekron. Baal Zebub was a Semitic god that was adopted by the Philistine

---

18. Van der Toorn, "Theology, Priests, and Worship," 3:2045.
19. For further study on the god Dagon see: Healey, "Dagon," In *DDD*, 216–19.

Ekronites. The word Zebub means "flies" in Hebrew, which is also found in Ugaritic, Akkadian, Jewish Aramaic, and Syriac as well as other Semitic languages. Based on the "flies" meaning of Zebub, the name of the God was understood as "Lord of the flies." In other words, it was believed that he could cause diseases or cure them. We should point out that the appearance of the name Zebub together with Baal points to a local testimony of the Canaanite deity Baal. Baal of the flies is mentioned in extra biblical sources. In the New Testament, Baal-Zebub is mentioned several times (Matt 10:25; 12:24; Mark 3:22; Luke 11:15), while some of the manuscripts include it as Baal Zebul. In Ugaritic literature, Zebul is the epithet of Baal.[20]

The goddess Ashtoreth had a temple at Beth-shan (1Sam 31:8–13). The city of Beth-shan was a Canaanite city under the Philistines' control. The etymology of the name remains obscure. In its masculine form, it is the name of the planet Venus, and it was then extended to the feminine form.[21] The goddess Ashtoreth was the principal goddess of Beth-shan; it was there that the armor of Saul hung on its temple walls. This corresponds to the Egyptian epigraphic and iconographic evidence as the war-goddess she was. It is noteworthy, that the names Baal and Ashtoreth appear together numerous times in the Hebrew Bible, which raises the possibility that it refers to gods and goddesses in general.[22]

A Philistine temple discovered at Tell Qasile, apparently first built in 1150 BCE, was rebuilt several times. The temple contains Aegean and Canaanite motifs, plus many objects associated with ritual objects such as a bird-shaped vessel and an incense altar. In houses and small shrines in Ashdod, several clay figurines of male and female were found, which is believed to be pairs of deities. In addition, an image of a female deity with small breasts, merged into a high-backed chair was discovered. The name of the deity is unknown, nevertheless, she is referred as "Ashdoda." Cult vessels were found in Ashdod, Ekron, Gezer, and Megiddo. As mentioned previously, these vessels are known as *kernos*, which is a hollow pottery ring on which objects like birds or pomegranates are set, reflecting Aegean influences. It is not clear how it was used, but most likely, a liquid was poured into the ring and used for libation. In ancient Greece, *kernos* was used primarily in the cults of Demeter and Kore, found in Cybele and Attis. Another type of container for fluids used for drinking or pouring

---

20. For further study on Baal Zebub see: Herrmann, "Baal Zebub," In *DDD*, 154–56.
21. Yahuda, "Meaning of the Name Esther," 174–78.
22. For the divine name Astrate see: Wyatt, "Astarte," In *DDD*, 109–14.

was the one-handled lion rhyton, which was found in places such as Tell Jerishe, Megiddo, Tell es-Safi, Tell Qasile, and Ekron. This is the Philistine equivalent to the Greek rhyton, which is a drinking horn, made of pottery or metal having a base in the form of the head of a woman or an animal.

Philistine priests are mentioned only once when the ark was captured and taken to Ashdod (1Sam 5). The Bible says that the priests of Dagon did not enter the house of Dagon because they found Dagon had fallen on his face before the ark of Yahweh. The Bible also mentions that the Philistines took idols into battle (2Sam 5:21). It was customary in the ancient world to bring the gods to the battle in order to insure divine assistance. Indeed, the Israelites brought the ark of Yahweh to the battle at Eben-ezer. Following the battle, the victorious side would carry the gods of the enemy as a sign of the superiority of their god.[23] To celebrate their victory over Saul, the Philistines carried Saul's head and his armor. They placed Saul's armor in the temple of their god Dagon. Similarly, David and his men carried the idols of the Philistines to display their victory. In contrast to the passage from 2Samuel (5:21), 1 Chronicles (14:12) says that David ordered troops to burn the Philistines' idols. This is what Deuteronomy 7:25 tells the Israelites to do: "As for the images of their gods, you will consign them to fire."

In addition to priests, the Bible also mentions Philistines' diviners. Since God inflicted the Philistines with plagues, the priests and the diviners suggested they should compensate the God of Israel. They needed to send five golden tumours and five golden mice as a guilt offering to God (1Sam 6:4). This compensation served as a protection against further suffering. The significance of the number five is that the Philistines had five city states. As for the shape of the images as tumours and mice, they served as a confession that the tumours and the mice from which they suffered had been sent by God. It is possible that behind the images, we have homeopathic principle curing like with like. This resembles the making of the bronze serpent (Num 21), however, there the serpent is the agent of healing.[24]

Conclusion

In conclusion, it is believed that the Philistines came from Capthorim, which is identified with the isle of Crete. It was suggested that the tribe of Dan originated with the Philistines. This tribe's members were seafarers worshipping

23. Miller and Roberts, *The hand of the Lord*, 9–16
24. Gordon, *1 & 2 Samuel*, 101.

the sun where they lived by the eastern Mediterranean coast in the Jaffa area. However, the similarities between the two groups can be explained as the outcome of contact and influence. More so, excavation at Tel Dan reveals that there were no signs of Philistine pottery. This evidently shows that the Danites belonged to the Israelites and not to the Sea People's confederation.

The battles between the Israelites and the Philistines are first mentioned in the Book of Judges. It was during Samuel's period that the Philistines reached the height of their power. Saul, in spite of several successful wars with the Philistines, lost the last battle against the Philistines at Mount Gilboa, which led to his death. Following this battle, the Philistines gained control over all of the north and central parts of Israel as well as west of the Jordan. It was only King David who finally succeeded in defeating the Philistines who later served in his army.

The Philistine confederacy was ruled by the *seranim*. During the time of crisis they would meet and decide together on what action to take. The *seranim* who ruled the Philistines also served as commanders of the army. The military forces of the Philistines were well organized; they were composed of infantry, archers, chariotry, and horseman. As for livelihood, their environment provided them with the ability to become skilled maritime workers and agrarians.

No written documents that might refer to the Philistine language were ever found. Examination of the Hebrew Bible shows there are several words that point to the Philistine origin. It appears that the Israelites and the Philistines were communicating freely. They probably were using a Canaanite dialect. The fact that the Philistines were influenced by their new place of habitat is also evident in their religion. The Philistines replaced their gods with male gods from the Canaanite Pantheon.

Philistine priests are mentioned only once, as are the philistine diviners. Several ritual objects were found at Ashdod and Gezer, which are related to objects from the Aegean area. Cult vessels were found in Ashdod, Ekron, Gezer, and Megiddo, and they were used for libation.

Following the description of the Philistine material culture, we turn to the last chapter describing the tragic downfall of our hero Samson at the hands of the Philistines.

8

The Death of Samson

RAMBAN, IN HIS COMMENTARY on Genesis 49:18 says that Samson was the only judge among all the judges of Israel who fell into the hands of his enemies. When Jacob foresaw in his prophecy that Samson would not complete his mission against the Philistines, he prayed to God saying: "I wait for Your deliverance, O Lord!" because only God's salvation is eternal. It is believed that Jacob's words echo the disappointment of Samson's fate.[1] As previously mentioned, the portrayal of Samson shows that he was a unique judge like no other judge mentioned in the Book of Judges. Thus, not surprisingly, even his death is described with exceptional details. The last part of Samson's life is narrated in chapter 16:23–31. This section can be divided into three parts: 1) Verses 23–27 describes the Philistine's jubilation at Samson fall; 2) Verses 28–30 Samson's revenge and his death; 3) Verse 31 the burial of Samson with a formula ending. Hence, in the current chapter we examine each of these segments. We will study the Philistine's jubilation, which included two short poems, one by the *seranim* and the second by the people. The poem by the *seranim* was partially repeated by the people. So what do the poems try to convey and how different are they? In the second part we describe Samson's revenge, which is preceded by a prayer to God. Therefore, we compare it to his first prayer to God at Ramath-lehi and see how different the prayers are. In his prayer, Samson expressed a death wish; therefore, we judge it against other death wishes and their outcome. Finally, we describe Samson's burial and the special language that was used to describe it. Was there any significance to his burial site? And why does the narrator mention for a second time that Samson judged Israel for 20 years?

1. *Gen. R. 98:19; 99:12.*

The Death of Samson

The Philistines' Jubilation

Samson was brought down to Gaza where he became a mill slave in prison. He was preforming tasks that were done by animals; this was to humiliate him. To celebrate their victory over Samson, the Philistine made a great sacrifice to their god Dagon. They praised him for delivering Samson into their hands. When their hearts were merry from eating and drinking, they called for Samson to come out of the prison house so he could entertain them. They amused themselves watching him suffer. This is the background of the last encounter between Samson and the Philistines. It takes place in the palace of Dagon the Philistine god. A new dimension is added to our story: a feud between Samson's God and the Philistine god. This motif would be repeated later in the Book of Samuel, which describes the battle between Israel and the Philistines.

Before describing the Philistines' jubilation, the narrator starts with a report that Samson's hair started to grow, which hints to the rejuvenation of Samson's power. Nevertheless, in spite of the growth of the hair, the author later stressed the fact that Samson turned to God in prayer (v.28). Turning to God in prayer is similar to the previous episode at En-hakkore of Lehi, where Samson turned to God in prayer. So why does the author mention the hair? It appears that by mentioning the hair, the author had two objectives in mind. First he connected this section with the segment of Samson and Delilah and the birth narrative. And second he diminished the magical nature of the hair and instead showed the superiority of prayer.[2]

It was through his prayer that Samson achieved his last victory against the Philistines. The prayer shows his dependence on God. More so, it appears that Samson was aware of his faith. He turned to God to remember him and to give him strength for the last time. This is in contrast to the episode of En-hakkore of Lehi, where the prayer was in the form of complaints and resentment. Here, he asks for God's mercy. By God answering Samson's prayer, the narrator shows that his powers were from God and he was a tool in the hands of providence.

The Philistines celebrated their victory at the temple of their deity Dagon. Temples that are dedicated to the god Dagon existed at Gaza, Ashdod and Beth-Shean (Judg 16:23; 1Sam 5:1–7; 1Chr10:10).[3] As noted in

---

2. Amit, *Judges*, 305–06.
3. According to the Book of Maccabees the temple in Ashdod was destroyed by the Hasmonean Jonathan (1Mac 10:83–4).

the previous chapter, Dagon was an important and widely worshiped deity in the Ancient Near East. The Philistines adopted Dagon as their god after their settlement in Canaan. The fact that Samson was brought to the temple of Dagon, the god of grain, is ironic since Samson burned the grain and the fields of the Philistines. By bringing him to their temple, the Philistines ascribe Samson's downfall to their god, not to the Almighty. It's noteworthy that in the Hebrew Bible there is a current motif that describes an Israelite in the dungeon. Following the incarceration the Israelite is elevated in status. This was the case with Joseph (Gen 41) and Daniel (1–6). In the Samson story the reverse is true; Samson is led from the dungeon to his death.

The Philistines expressed their jubilation by uttering a short poem with a repeated rhythm:

> "*Our* god has delivered into *our* hands
> *Our* enemy Samson"

This short poem was sung by the *seranim*. Their gathering was accompanied by a great sacrifice to their god Dagon. The Philistines did not turn to the aid of their god Dagon. However, since they captured Samson, they attributed their success to their god. By mentioning their god, they added a religious dimension to the story. Samson is not only the enemy of the Philistines, he is also the enemy of their god. The belief that their god is behind their victory is not limited to the Philistines. Indeed, we find that the Israelites also attributed their victories to their God: "So the Lord our God also delivered into our power King Og of Bashan, with all his men, and we dealt them such a blow that no survivor was left" (Deut 3:3). When the spies return from Jericho they said: "The Lord has delivered the whole land into our power; in fact all the inhabitants of the land are quaking before us" (Josh 2:24).

The word *our* is a key word in verse 23and it is repeated three times: *Our* god has delivered into *our* hands *our* enemy Samson. The fact that it is repeated here three times, as well as three times in the next verse, (v.24) strengthens the perception that this was a song that was chanted. The Philistines appear here as a chorus. This form of singing by a large group of people was also prevalent among the Israelites. When God delivered the Israelites from the Egyptians and the Israelites crossed the sea, Moses and the Israelites sang to the Lord (Exod 15). When God gave the Israelites water, they sang a song at the well (Num 21:17). Following David's victory over Goliath, the women sang: "Saul has slain his thousands; David, his tens of thousands" (1Sam.18:7;21:12; 29:5).

The Death of Samson

After the poem that the *seranim* sang, we find a second poem that the people sang. The sight of Samson caused major jubilation. Samson is not only the enemy of the *seranim*, he is also the enemy of all Philistine people. Hence they sang:

> "*Our* god has delivered into *our* hands
> The enemy who devastated *our* land
> And who slew so many of us" (Judg 16:24).

This poem is longer than the poem sang by the *seranim*. As a matter of fact, the first poem was an abbreviated form and the second one is the expansion. Hence, the people repeated the poem sung by the *seranim*, "*Our* god has delivered into *our* hands." These are the same words that were sung by the *seranim* but with one slight change, instead of the last part "*Our* enemy Samson" they changed the words to "the enemy." This kind of change is typical in biblical poetry. But more importantly, while the *seranim* only state that Samson was their enemy, here the people elaborate and describe the destruction that was caused by Samson. In their poem, the Philistines accused Samson of two crimes: he ruined their land and caused many deaths. This refers to the story about the foxes and the story of the ass's jaw. Why didn't the *seranim* mention those events? We believe that it was too painful for them to admit their failure, they were humiliated severely by Samson, therefore, they stressed only the triumph over Samson. Noteworthy here is how the Philistines ended their poem in the past tense, "who slew so many of us." In other words, they are certain and confident that Samson will not be able to kill them anymore. However, this was wishful thinking since Samson will kill many of them later.

The Philistines brought Samson to amuse themselves (v.25). It appears that this verse should be placed before verse 24 since in that verse we read "when the people saw him." In other words, they could not see him before he was brought to them. ". . . Their spirit rose. . ." when Samson was brought to their palace, this expression refers to drinking wine, which appears on other occasions in the Hebrew Bible.[4] The call to bring Samson for entertainment has some similarities to King Ahasuerus story. According to the story, the king was merry with wine, he ordered Queen Vashti to come forth to display her beauty (Esth 1:10–11). In both stories the drinking resulted in bad judgment.[5]

---

4. 2Sam 13:28; Esth 1:10.
5. Zakovitz, *Life of Samson*, 199.

The Samson Story

The sight of their enemy faltering and fumbling caused the Philistines to break out in great laughter. To describe Samson entertaining his audience, the Bible says ויצחק לפניהם *wayeśaḥēq lipnêhem*—the JPS translated it as Samson was dancing for the Philistines.[6] All along, the Philistines wanted to make Samson helpless (Judg 16:5, 6, 19) and they achieved it. They humiliated Samson by bringing him to the palace of their god Dagon. This recalls a similar situation with King Saul. After the last battle at Mount Gilboa when Saul and his sons died, the Philistines stripped him and carried off his head and his armor. They placed his armor in the temple of their god and they impaled his head in the temple of Dagon (1Chrn 10:10).

There was a pause in the entertainment that Samson provided to the Philistines. Hence, the narrator describes to us that the Philistines put Samson between the pillars at the center of the building. Why they did so is not clear. It is possible that they stationed him at the center of the temple so people would have a good view of Samson. The Excavation at Tell Qasile shows remains of a temple in Stratum X. Two pillars supporting the roof were integral parts of the temple construction.[7] The mention of the pillars here is foreshadowing the future. It is also a reminder to the reader of Samson's previous heroic deeds, where pillars also played a role when he carried the gates of Gaza.

Because Samson was blind, he had an escort who held him by his hand. Samson asked him to lead him so he could feel the pillars the temple rested on. In the previous verse (v.25), the pillars were already mentioned, but here the narrator says these were the pillars that the temple rested on. This detail is significant for a person who wants to topple the pillars of the temple and not to lean on them. Samson is portrayed here as helpless; he is blind and needs help. This is in contrast to his past when all along he fought his battles with no aid. Nevertheless, Samson who was passive so far and did as he was told by the Philistines, then took initiative. He ordered the boy who was leading him to guide him, so he could feel the pillars in order to lean on them. The boy who guided Samson is a secondary character and his role is limited exclusively to this verse—he neither appears before nor after.[8] According to Josephus, Samson concealed from the boy his true purpose, hence he says: "And he, deeming it direr than all his ills to be unable to

---

6. The same expression is used with David as he was "dancing before Yahweh" (2Sam 6:21).

7. Mazar, "A Philistine Temple," 42:48.

8. Zakovitz, *Life of Samson*, 201.

The Death of Samson

avenge of such insults, induced the boy who led him by the hand—telling him that from weariness he needed a stay whereon to rest—to conduct him close to the columns."[9] It's noteworthy that Josephus omits the words "the pillars that the temple rests upon"; again this was done in order to conceal his true plan from the boy.

Meanwhile, there is a pause by the narrator. He describes a packed temple with men and women and the Philistine seranim in attendance. In addition, there were 3,000 people on the roof, all of them were watching Samson dance. So far, we read in verses 23, 24, 27 about the Philistines' deeds, and in verses 25–26 about Samson's actions. Now the narrator breaks from his pattern and describes the temple and the celebration that is taking place. This is done in order to increase the tension and the magnitude of Samson's act. According to our verse, not only was the temple full of men and woman, additionally there were 3,000 people on the roof. As we mentioned previously, the numbers of Samson's enemies increased from episode to episode. Since, 3,000 refers only to the people on the roof, the sage's exaggerated, and "R. Levi said: It is written, *And there were upon the roof about three thousand men and women* (v.27). These were the number on the edge of the roof, but no one knows how many were behind them."[10]

Samson's Revenge

Samson's revenge and his death are described in verses 28–30. Samson uttered a short prayer to God. He pleaded for God's help for one last display of strength that would help him take vengeance against the Philistines. In contrast to his first prayer to God at Ramath-lehi, where he referred to God by the pronoun You (Jud15:18), here in his second prayer to God, Samson uttered the divine name twice, O Lord God. This divine title is rarely used in the Torah (Gen15:2, 8; Deut 3:24; 9:26). It is used in a context of complaint prayer and request. He asked God to remember him for the personal wrong he was suffering. In his plea to God, he asks to *strengthen* him *just this once*. In other words, this is his last request from God. The same language *just this once* is also found in Abraham's plea on behalf of the people of Sodom and Gomorrah after several attempts to persuade God (Gen 18:32); as well as for Gideon when he requests a sign for a second time from God (Judg 6:39). Like Abraham and Gideon's pleas, Samson also appeals to precedent.

9. Josephus, *Antiquities* 5.315.
10. *Gen. R.* 98:14.

God has strengthened him in the past, now he asks him for the last time, and he would not trouble God anymore. Furthermore, he asks God to remember him. The motif of remembrance is recurring many times in the Hebrew Bible. It implies faithfulness to the covenant between God and his people. Samson is calling on God to act based on the special relationship he has with God; he is a Nazirite of God even before he was born.

Since Samson's eyes were gouged, he asks for revenge on the Philistines: "if only for one of my two eyes." (16:28). In other words, the death of the Philistines would atone for the cruelty exacted upon him. Not clear, however, is why Samson mentioned only one eye. Why didn't he ask for revenge for the loss of two eyes? We find an answer in the Midrash:

> "R. Aha answered: He begged from Him: 'Sovereign of the Universe! Grant me reward for my loss of one eye in this world, and let the reward for my loss of the other one be kept ready for me in the hereafter."[11]

The narrator does not tell the reader that God harkened to Samson's prayer, but his actions show that his prayer was answered. Samson grasped the two main pillars that supported the roof, and then bending forward, he forced them out of the perpendicular. Feeling that he regained his strength he said: "let me die with the Philistine" (v. 30). This is not a request, but it is a cheering cry that resulted with the death of thousands of Philistines. Ironically, blind, chained, and ridiculed, as he died, Samson killed more Philistines than in his entire life, ending his life in a dramatic fashion. Usually people achieve more during their lifetime, but with Samson we find the reverse. The measure of Samson's success is the number of causalities he inflicted on the Philistines. Samson dies according to his own wish. Samson's desire to die was compared to some of the fables from ancient times, in particular, the fable of the wasp and the snake.

> "A WASP seated himself upon the head of a Snake and, striking him unceasingly with his stings, wounded him to death. The Snake, being in great torment and not knowing how to rid himself of his enemy, saw a wagon heavily laden with wood, and went and purposely placed his head under the wheels, saying, "At least my enemy and I shall perish together."[12]

---

11. *Num. R.* 9.24.
12. *Aesop's fable*, no.193

The Death of Samson

In another fable we read:

> "A tuna fish who was being chased by a dolphin was splashing madly through the water. Just when the dolphin was about to catch him, the tuna fish heaved himself forward with a great effort and landed on an island. Matching his effort, the dolphin ran aground beside him. The tuna fish then turned to look at the gasping dolphin and said, 'I do not grieve over my own death, so long as I am able to see that the one to blame is dying together with me!' *The fable shows that people readily undergo a disaster when they can witness the destruction of those who are to blame.*[13]

In his first prayer to God, Samson asked for his life and he was revived. By contrast, his second prayer asked for his death and his wish was granted. This is the only time in the Hebrew Bible that such a wish was granted. The Bible mentions other heroes who implored God to end their lives. We read about Moses (Num11:10–15), Elijah (1Kgs 19:4), Jeremiah (20:17), and Jonah.[14] However, God refused these heroes requests and they continued with their mission.[15]

According to the Midrash, the reason for Samson's harsh punishment is because "Samson went after his eyes; therefore the Philistines put out his eyes, as it said, and the Philistines laid hold on him and put out his eyes."[16] It's noteworthy that when David is chosen to be the king of Israel, God said to Samuel: "For not as man sees [does the Lord see]; a man sees only what is visible, but the Lord sees into the heart" (1Sam 16:7). In other words, God can see all, but man's vision is limited. Ironically, as long as Samson could see, he was "blind" to his own deeds; it was only when the Philistines put out his eyes that he became aware of his weakness. Still, the sages tried to balance the harsh verdict that Samson received by saying: "Rav said: Samson said before the Holy One Blessed is He: Master of the Universe! Remember for me the twenty two years that I judged Israel and I did not even say to them, 'Bring a staff for me from one place to another place.'"[17] It was noted that this Midrash is similar to Samuel's speech: "Whose ox have I taken, or whose ass have I taken? From whose hand have I taken a bribe to

---

13. *Aesop's Fables*, no.160
14. Greenstein, "Riddle of Samson," 242.
15. Olson, "Judges," In *NIB* 2:860.
16. *Soṭah*. 9b.
17. Ibid., 10a.

look the other way" (1Sam 12: 3).[18] Samson says further, as recorded in the Gemarah, that he was careful not to accept bribes. Therefore, the loss of the eyes could not be attributed to bribery "which blinds the eyes of the wise" (Duet 16:19). More so, the Midrash praises Samson for acting alone in his wars and not using his people.

The Burial of Samson

The narrator ends the last part our story by mentioning that his brothers and his entire father's house came to pick up his body. This is the first time that we hear that he had brothers. It shows that they respected their brother. Abravanel pointed out that Samson's mother was barren, but after she bore Samson she also had other sons, as in the case of Hannah the mother of Samuel (1Sam 2:21). Alternatively, mentioning brothers refers to Samson's family. As for his father's household, this refers to the rest of his father's tribe.

The verse that ends the Samson cycle brings us back to the beginning, the story of his birth.[19] As Samson was passive in his birth, so he is after his death. His family members are acting here and burying him. The description of carrying Samson and bringing him to his burial site is reminiscent of the burial of Jacob: "all of Joseph's household, his brothers, and his father's household . . . His sons carried him to the land of Canaan, and buried him in the cave of the field of Machpelah, and the field near Mamre, which Abraham had bought for burial site from Ephron the Hittite." (Gen 50:8,13).[20]

The family buried Samson between Zorah and Eshtaol at the tomb of his father Manoah. Hence, signaling reconciliation between the family and Samson. By declaring the site of his burial, the story returns to the opening stage of our story. There it says that the spirit of God seized Samson between Zorah and Eshtaol. As in the Samson story, an identical site for his election and burial appears also in the Gideon story. Gideon and Samson were elected and died at the same site. Hence, Gideon was elected at Ophrah of the Abi-ezrites, the place where he was later buried in the grave of his father Joash (Jud 8:31).

There is a final note that says that he judged Israel for 20 years. A similar statement appeared already at the end of chapter 15. According to Abravanel, the statement in chapter 15 refers to Samson's spiritual demise,

18. Glendar "Samson is upon you," 71.
19. Zakovitz, *Life of Samson*, 209.
20. Ibid.

The Death of Samson

which began at that point, but when mentioned in our chapter, it refers to his physical death. A similar interpretation is given by Radak who says that Samson's tenure lasted for 20 years. It was first mentioned after his exploit at En-hakkorei because it was there that his downfall began. Until that time he enjoyed God's help, but from that point on, he began to stray because of temptations and his end was a matter of time. We should point out that repetition was one of the tools that was used by the Biblical narrator. The repetition had several functions among them to show the difference between the different parts of the story. Noteworthy is that the sages believed that Samson's judgeship lasted far after his death. According to them, his frightening memory held the Philistines in check for another 20 years. The Bible says at the end of the other judges' lives "that the land was tranquil for forty years," not so with Samson because he did not complete the deliverance of Israel from the hand of the Philistines.

Among modern scholars, Kaufman suggested that the editor wanted to stress the existence of two cycles in the Samson story. The first cycle describes Samson's heroic actions, which end in chapter 15. The second one, which is found in chapter 16, contains descriptions of Samson's heroism but not in the battlefields. To express this idea, the editor uses similar statements at the end of chapters 15 and 16.[21] Budda, on the other hand, suggested that the Deuteronomist did not approve the traditions that are found in chapter 16 such as Samson going to a harlot, falling in a trap by Delilah and her people and the description of his death. Therefore, he removed those traditions and ended the story in 15:20. However, a later "liberal" editor inserted those rejected traditions back to the Samson story and ended it with a final note in 16:31. This was done without removing the pervious ending of chapter 15.[22] This suggestion by Budda removes the difficulties in the text. However, questions need to be asked. If this is the case, why did the Deuteronomist not remove the tradition about Jephthah the Gileadite who was a son of a harlot or the fact that he sacrificed his daughter? (Judg 11:1, 30–40)

It is strange that Samson is referred to as a judge. His deeds and actions show otherwise. He was a single hero who did not lead his people into a battle against a national enemy or oppressor. His battles are motivated by his personal agenda. At the end of his era, the land of Israel was not tranquil but was in the state of anarchy. His actions were temporary solutions to

---

21. Kaufman, *Judges*, 260.

22. Budda, *Judges*, 91–2, 104; According to Boling, chapter 16 is one of the seventh-century additions, see: Boling, *Judges*, 136, 252–53.

the battle against the Philistines. The anarchy that is described in the Book of Judges serves as a pretext to the Book of Samuel, which starts with the oppression of the Philistines. It was this anarchy and the oppression of the Philistines that ultimately led to the new area of the Israelite history; the inauguration of Saul as the first King of Israel.

Conclusion

As a judge, Samson failed to carry the mission that was assign to him by God, and he brought destruction upon himself. His demise is described in minute detail, which is not found with the other judges. The Philistines' jubilation of the capture of Samson is expressed by a short poem with repeated rhythm. In the poem, the Philistine *seranim* attribute their victory to their god Dagon. The people repeated the poem sung by the *seranim* and describe the destruction that was caused by Samson. The Philistines ended their poem with words that show their confidence; that Samson will not be able to kill them anymore. In his prayer to God, Samson expressed his wish for death, which is different from his first prayer for victory. He ends his life in a dramatic fashion, which resulted in the death of thousands of Philistines. Samson is the only one in the Hebrew Bible whose death wish is granted. Samson's desire to die has similarities to some of the fables from ancient times. Samson was buried by his family members, which shows that they respected him. They buried him between Zorah and Eshtaol at the tomb of his father Manoah. By mentioning the site of his burial, the story returns to the opening stage of our story. There it says that the spirit of God seized Samson between Zorah and Eshtaol.

Conclusion

THE SAMSON STORY BEGINS with his birth and tragically ends with his death with no continuation. Three times the narrator said that Samson was a judge and deliverer destined to save Israel from the Philistines (Judg 13:5; 15:20; 16:31). However, the story shows that Samson did not deliver his people. He is the last judge and he failed, dying with his enemies. He fought single-handedly against the Philistines without an army. His fights were personal vendettas and had nothing to do with any national crisis. More so, even his own people surrendered him to the Philistines (15:13). This failure would lead to a future change where the institution of Judgeship would be replaced by Kingship.

No other judge receives so much attention and detailed description in the Book of Judges. The narrator chose to describe Samson as a hero with supernatural strength, which reminds the readers of the Greek mythical heroes. This is not a coincidence, because the Israelites were living in the vicinity of the Philistines and were familiar with their culture. Nevertheless, in spite of the similarity to mythical heroes the narrator demythologizes Samson's image and transforms his persona to suit his monotheistic views. The opening scene with the announcement of the birth of Samson reminds us of various myths about sexual relations between gods and daughters of men that were prevalent in the ancient world. Hence, in contrast to ancient myths, Samson is not a son of God, and his father and mother are both humans who received a divine message about the birth of their son. The story about Samson's birth gives us the answer about the origin of this super-human being. Samson is a Nazarite from the womb. It is the Nazarite vow that God imposed on Samson's mother that is behind his strength. The usage of the Nazirite vow and the motif of hair came to de-mythologize the image of Samson. Not a mythical hero, but an Israelite hero who received his power from God.

The Samson Story

Reading the Samson stories reveals that there are three major blocks to the story. Hence, it was suggested that the various tales about Samson were initially told separately and only afterward collected and arranged to create a story about the hero named Samson. However, investigation of the Samson story shows otherwise. The story is a masterful piece of work that was written by a skillful writer. It is homogenous and describes the life of Samson from his birth to his death. Events are narrated in sequence and are connected to each other. More so, some of the stories are linked to previous stories in the Hebrew Bible and are based on them. The stories also show affinities to the Book of Samuel, which continues to describe the battles against the Philistines. Any attempt to eliminate or alter parts of the story will damage the continuity, harmony, unity, and logical structure of the story.

One of the themes that repeats itself in the Samson stories is his involvement with the foreign women. The women have a central role in Samson's life. They serve as the glue to the whole Samson story; without them there is no story. Samson's involvement with them serves as an excuse for killing the Philistines and puts the story in motion. It is God who initiated this relationship. These foreign women have the upper hand and bring Samson to his downfall. The three women—the Timnite the harlot, and Delilah—are the subject of his sexual desires. The Timnite and Delilah both yielded to the pressure of their own people and mutually betrayed Samson. Only the name of the third women is given—her name is Delilah. The first two women, the Timnite and the harlot, remain nameless. Samson did not exhibit any emotion toward the first two women. It is the third woman, Delilah, to whom Samson showed his emotion—he loved her. Falling in love with Delilah diverted him from God's plan, which saw his involvement with the women as a pretext to fighting with the Philistines. With Delilah, he was involved emotionally, which led to his downfall and to his tragic death.

In the ancient world, riddles were a source of entertainment, especially at banquets and celebrations in the king's court: They were a test of wisdom. Therefore, not surprisingly, during the festivities celebrating his marriage, Samson entertains the Philistines with a riddle and challenges them to solve it within the seven days of the wedding celebration. It was suggested that Samson's riddle is independent and is not connected to the narrative. Both the riddle and its answer are older than the biblical story, which led to creation of the slain lion story and eating the honey from its carcass. However,

Conclusion

this is not the case, since Samson's riddle in its current form is based on his adventure with the lion. The riddle describes his two trips to Timnah. In his first trip he killed a lion, and in the second he ate honey from the carcass of the lion. The Philistines answered Samson's riddle indirectly to imply that they discovered the solution on their own. Their answer shows that they responded only to the second part of the riddle and not the first part. They explain "strong" and "sweet" but not "eater" and "food." The answer that the Philistines gave in interrogatory form suggests that we have a second riddle here. The riddle speaks about love, which is stronger than a lion and sweeter than honey. Samson accepted their interpretation. He knew that it was his wife who gave them the interpretation to his riddle, as he alluded to it in his response to them. In his response, Samson used imagery from the world of farmers; he refers to his wife allegorically as a heifer and the companions as the ones who used her for plowing. In other words, Samson was suspicious that she slept with one of them, thereby, revealing the secret of the riddle. More so, since the theme of love and sexuality was the subject of the Philistines' answer (riddle), we can say that his answer was a description of a sexual act.

The Philistine's mythological heroes are the gods or sons of gods. Their strength lies in their divine origin. They are fighting against gods and sons of gods, demons, and dragons. On the other hand, Samson is a human with super strength and fights against the Philistines who are real people. Samson's strength originated from God who gave Samson the power to slay the lion bare-handed, to kill 30 people at Ashkelon, to break the ropes that the men of Judah tied him up with, and to kill 1,000 men with a jawbone. After his victory at Lehi, Samson acknowledged that it was God who was responsible for his triumph. More so, before his final act, Samson prayed to God to give him strength and God answered his prayer. The Hebrews lived in the vicinity of the Philistines and probably were familiar with the Philistines myth about gods, and demigods who fought among themselves and against demons and dragons. The Israelite monotheistic religion had to cope with it. Therefore, not surprisingly, the Bible described Samson's acts with some similarity to the Philistine's mythical heroes. However, the Biblical narrator de-mythologized those stories by stripping them of the mythological elements. Instead it describes an earthly hero, Samson, who defeats his enemy and by doing so showed the superiority of the Israelite God over the Philistines' gods.

The Samson Story

The Philistines whom Samson fought from his birth to his death came from Capthorim, which is identified as the isle of Crete. Pottery that was found in their places of habitat point to "Philistines' pottery," which has common motifs with the Mycenean culture, which is the place scholars believed they originated from. In spite of the similarities between the Philistines and the tribe of Dan, the Danites did not belong to the Sea Peoples confederation. The similarities can be explained as an outcome of contact and influence. The Philistine confederacy included five major cities ruled by the *seranim* who also served as commanders of the army. Their military forces were well organized and were composed of infantry, archers, chariots, and horsemen. These tools gave them major advantages in their battles against the Israelites. The Philistines controlled the sea and the land trades between Canaan and the Mediterranean world. They become skilled maritime workers and agrarians. No written documentation referring to Philistine language has been found. The Samson stories show that the Israelites and the Philistines were communicating freely. The Philistines probably were speaking a Canaanite dialect. As for their religion, several ritual objects were found by archeologists at the Philistines' cities, which are related to objects from the Aegean. Nevertheless, the Philistines not only acquired the local language but they replaced their gods with male gods from the Canaanite Pantheon. Hence, we find that they worshipped Dagon, Baal-zebub, and the goddess Ashtoret.

Even in his death, Samson was different from the other judges. The Bible gives us an elaborate description of his final days. The Philistines celebrated the capture of their enemy Samson in the temple of their god Dagon. To express their jubilation, they utter two short poems: one by the *seranim* and the second one by the people. In the poems, they attributed their success in capturing Samson to their god Dagon. Chained, ridiculed, and his eyes gouged out, Samson asked God for a last display of strength that would help him take vengeance against the Philistines. His wish was granted resulting in the death of thousands of Philistines. The story ends with the burial of Samson in his father's grave between Zorah and Eshtaol. By mentioning the site of Samson's burial, the story returns to the opening stage where the spirit of God originally seized Samson—between Zorah and Eshtaol.

Reading the Samson story, the impression is that the narrator wanted to prepare the reader for the next stage of the Israelite history, which is the kingship. Therefore, the narrator described the chaos that existed in the

CONCLUSION

Judge's period. In his view, Samson exemplifies the notion of: "In those days there was no king in Israel everyone did as he pleased" (Judg17:10; 18:1; 19:1; 21:25).

Bibliography

Achard, Robert Martin. *From Death to Life*. Translated by Joseph Penny Smith. Edinburgh and London: Oliver and Boyd, 1960.
Ackerman, S. *Warrior Dancer, Seductress, Queen: Women in Judges and Biblical Texts*. New York: Doubleday, 1988.
Aesop's Fables. Translated by Laura Gibbs. Oxford: Oxford University Press, 2002.
Albright, W.F. "Some Canaanite- Phoenician Sources of Hebrew Wisdom." *VTSuppl* 3(1955) 1-15.
———. *The Archaeology of Palestine*. Harmondsworth: Penguin, 1949.
Alter, R. "How Conventions Help Us Read: The Case of the Bible's Annunciation Type -Scene." *Proof* 3(1983) 115-30.
Amit, Yairah. *The Book of Judges: The Art of Editing*. Translated by Jonathan Chipman. Leiden: Brill, 1999.
———. *Judges: Introduction and Commentary*. Tel Aviv: Am Oved, 1999. (Hebrew)
Andersen Francis I and David Noel Freedman. *Amos*. AB 24 A. New York: Doubleday, 1989.
Apollodorus. *The Library*. Translated by James George Frazer. Cambridge Massachusetts: Harvard University Press, 1921.
Assis, Elie. "The Significance of the Narrative Concerning the Annunciation of Samson's Birth (Judg 13)." *Shnaton* 15(2005) 21-38.
Attridge Harold W and Robert A. Oden. *Philo of Byblos: The Phoenician History*. Washington, DC: The Catholic Biblical Association of America, 1981.
Bal, M. *Lethal Love: Feminist Literary Readings of Biblical Love Stories*. Bloomington: Indiana University Press, 1987.
Bar, Shaul. "The Punishment of Burning in the Hebrew Bible." *OTE* 25 (2012) 27-39.
———. *A letter that Has Not Been Read: Dreams in the Hebrew Bible*. Cincinnati: HUC Press: 2001.
Barry G. Webb. *The Book of the Judges: an Integrated Reading*. JSOTSup, 46. Sheffield: JSOT, 1987.
Bartusch, Mark W. *Understanding Dan: An Exegetical Study of Biblical City, Tribe and Ancestor*. JSOT 379. London: Sheffield Academic Press, 2003.
Bauer, H. "Zu Simsons Rätsel in Richter Kapitel 14." *ZDMG* 66(1912) 473-74
Bentzen, Aage. *Introduction to the Old Testament*. Copenhagen: Gads, 1948.
Blank, S. H. "Riddle." In *IDB* 4:78-9.
Blenkinsopp, J. "Structure Style in Judges 13-16." *JBL* 82(1963) 65-76.
Block, Daniel I. *Judges, Ruth*. Nashville, Tennessee: Broadman & Holman, 1999.

Bibliography

Boling, Robert G. *Judges*. AB 6A. Garden City, New York: Doubleday, 1975.
Brettler, Marc Zvi. *The Book of Judges*. London: Rutledge, 2002.
Broida, Marian. "Closure in Samson." *Journal of Hebrew Scriptures* 10 (2010) 2-34.
Brooks, Simcha Shalom. "Saul and the Samson Narrative." *JSOT* 71(1996) 19-25.
Buber, M. *On the Bible*. Edited by Nahum N. Glatzer. New York: Schoken, 1968.
Budde, Karl D. *Das Buch Der Richter*. Leipzig und Tübingen: Freiburg I. B, 1897.
Burney, C.F. *The Book of Judges with Introduction and Notes*. 1903. Repr., New York: Ktav, 1970.
Butler, Trent C. *Judges*. WBC 8. Grand Rapids, Michigan: Zondervan, 2009.
Carus, P. *The Story of Samson and its Place in the Religious Development of Mankind*. Chicago: Open Court, 1907.
Cassuto, U. *The Goddess Anath*. Jerusalem: Bialik Institute, 1951. (Hebrew).
———. *A Commentary on the Book of Genesis*. Translated by Israel Abraham. Jerusalem: Magnes, 1961.
Chisholm, Robert B. "What's Wrong with this Picture? Stylistic Variation as a Rhetorical Technique in Judges." *JSOT* 34(2009) 171-182.
Civil, M. *The Farmer's Instructions: A Sumerian Agricultural Manual*. AOSup 5. Sabadell Barcelona: AUSA, 1994.
Cogan Mordechai and Tadmor Hayim. *II Kings*. AB 11. Garden City New York: Doubleday, 1988.
Cohen Simon. "Samson." In *UJE* 9:341-44.
Condos Theony. *Star Myths of the Greeks and Romans*. Grand Rapids, MI: Phanes, 1997.
Cook, G.A. *The Book of Ezekiel*. Edinburgh: T. & T. Clark, 1936.
Cornelius, I. "The Lion in the Art of the Ancient Near East: A Study of Selected Motifs." *JNSL* 15(1989) 53-85.
Crenshaw, J.L. *Samson: A Secret Betrayed, a Vow Ignored*. Atlanta: John Knox, 1978.
———. "Samson." In *ABD* (1992)5:950-54.
———. "The Samson Saga: Filial Devotion of Erotic Attachment?" *ZAW* 86(1974) 470-504.
Diodorus of Sicilly. Trans. C.H. Oldfather. Cambridge, Massachusetts: Harvard University Press, 1935.
Dothan, Trude. *The Philistines and their Material Culture*. New Haven and London: Yale University Press, 1982.
———. "Philistines." In *ABD* 5(1992) 328-33.
Dupont –Sommer, A. "Une Inscription phénicienne archaique récemment trouvée à Kition (Chypre)." *Académie des Inscriptions et Belles Letters, Mémoires*, 44(1970) 2-28.
Ehrlich, Arnold B. *Mikrâ Ki-Pheschutô*. New York: Ktav, 1969. (Hebrew).
Ehrlich, Carl S. *The Philistines in Transition: A History from 1000-730*. Leiden: E.J. Brill, 1996.
Eichrodt, Walter. *Theology of the Old Testament*. Translated by J. A. Baker. Philadelphia: Westminster, 1967.
Eisenstein, J. D. "Samson." In *Yisrael* 10:190-91.
Eissfeldt, O. "Die Rätsel in Jud 14." *ZAW* 30(1910) 132-35.
The Epic of Gilgamesh. Translated with an introduction by George, Andrew. London: Penguins Books, 2003.
Exum, J.C. "Promise and Fulfillment: Narrative Art in Judges 13." *JBL* 99(1980) 43-59.
———. "The Theological Dimension of the Samson Saga." *VT* 33(1983) 30-45

Bibliography

———. *Fragmented Women Feminist (Sub) versions of Biblical Narratives.* Sheffield: JSOT, 1993.
Fohrer, Georg. *Introduction to the Old Testament.* Translated by David E. Green. Nashville: Abingdon, 1968.
Frazer, James George. *The Fear of the Dead in Primitive Religion.* New York: Arno, 1977.
Gaster, Theodor H. *Myth Legend, and Custom in the Old Testament.* New York: Harper & Row, 1969.
Glender Shamai "Samson is upon you." *BethM* 51(2006) 63-71.
Gordon, C. H. "The Mediterranean Factor in the Old Testament." In *Congress Volume Bonn 1962*, edited by G.W. Anderson et al., 19-31. VTSup 9.Leiden: Brill, 196.
Gordon, Robert P. *1 & 2 Samuel: A Commentary.* Great Britain: Paternoster, 1986.
Gray, George Buchanan. *Numbers.* New York: Charles Scribner's sons, 1903.
Grayson, Albert Kirk. *Assyrian Royal Inscription.* Vol 2.Wiesbaden: Otto Harrassowitz, 1976.
Greene, Mark. "Enigma Variations: Aspects of the Samson Story (Judges 13-16)." *VE* 21(1991) 53-79.
Greenfield, J.C. "Philistines." In *IDB* 3:791-95.
Greenfield, J.C./ D. Sperling, "Philistines." In *EncJud* 16:52-5.
Greenstein, Edward L. "The Riddle of Samson." *Proof* 1(1981) 237-60.
Gressmann. H. *Die Anfänge Israels: (von 2. Mose bis Richter und Ruth): übersetzt., erklärt und mit Einleitungen versehen.* Göttingen: Vandenhoeck & Ruprecht, 1922.
Guillaume, Philippe. *Waiting for Josiah.* London: T&T Clark International, 2004.
Gunkel, H. 'Simson.' In *Reden und Aufsätze,* 38-64. Göttingen:Vandenhoeck & Ruprecht, 1913.
Harrison, R. K. *Introduction to the Old Testament.* Grand Rapids, Michigan: William B. Eerdmans, 1969.
Healey, J. F. "Dagon." In *DDD*, 216-19.
Herrmann, W. "Baal Zebub." In *DDD*, 154-56.
Hertzberg, H.W. *Die Bücher Josua, Richter, Ruth.* ATD, 9. Göttingen: Vandehoeck and Ruprecht, 1959.
Hyginus. *The Myth of Hyginus.* Translated and edited by Mary Grant. Lawrence: University of Kansas Publication, 1960.
Jacobson, Thorkild. *The Sumerian King List.* Chicago: University of Chicago Press, 1939.
Josephus, F. *Jewish Antiquities.* Translated by H. St. J. Thackeray. Cambridge, MA: Harvard University Press, 1930.
Vander Kam, James C. *Enoch and the Growth of the Apocalyptic Tradition.* Washington DC: The Catholic Biblical Association of America, 1984.
Kaufman, Y. *The Book of Judges.* Jerusalem: Kiryat Sepher, 1978. (Hebrew).
Kim, Jichan. *The Structure of the Samson Cycle.* Kampen: Kok Pharos, 1993.
Kitchen, K.A. "The Philistines." In *People of Old Testament Times*, edited by D. J. Wiseman, 53-78. Oxford: Clarendon, 1973.
Klein, Lillian R. *The Triumph of Irony in the Book of Judges.* JSOTSup 68. Sheffield: Almond, 1988.
Kopf , L. "Honey." *Tarbiz* 23(1952) 240-42.
Kraft, C. F. "Samson." In *IDB 4:198-201.*
Kratz, Reinhard G. *The Composition of the Narrative Books of the Old Testament.* Translated by John Bowden. New York: T&T Clark, 2005.
Lambert, W. G. "Enmeduranki and Related Matters." *JCS* 21(1967):126-38

BIBLIOGRAPHY

Licht, Jacob. *Commentary on the Book of Numbers (1-10)*. Jerusalem: Magnes, 1985. (Hebrew)

Lucian, *De Dea Syria*. Translated by Harold W. Attridge and Robert A. Oden. Missoula, Montana: Scholars Press, 1976.

Malamat, A. *Das davidische und salomonische Königreich und seine Beziehungen zu Ägypten und Syrien. Zur Entstenhung eines Grossreichs*. Österreichische Akademie der Wissenschaften, Philosophisch-historische Klasse, Sitzungsberichte, 407. Vienna: Österreichische Akademie der Wissenschaften, 1983.

Margalith, O. "More Samson Legends." *VT* 36(1986) 397-405.

———. "The Legends of Samson/Heracles." *VT* 37(1987) 63-70

———. "Samson's Riddle and Samson's Magic Locks." *VT* 36(1986) 225-34.

———. "The Parallel between the Samson story and the stories of the Aegean."*BethM* 27(1966) 122-30.

Mayer, G. "נזר nzr." In *TDOT* 9:306-11.

Mazar, A. "A Philistine Temple at Tell Qasile." *BA* 36(1973) 42-8.

McCarter, P. Kyle. *I Samuel*. Garden City, New York: Doubleday, 1980.

Milgrom, Jacob. *Numbers: The JPS Torah Commentary*. Philadelphia: The Jewish Publication Society, 1990.

Miller, Patrick D., Jr. *The Divine Warrior in Early Israel*. Harvard Semitic Monographs 5. Cambridge Massachusetts: Harvard University Press, 1973.

Miller, Patrick D., Jr. and J. J. M. Roberts. *The hand of the Lord. A Reassessment of the "Ark Narrative" of 1Samuel*. Baltimore: John Hopkins, 1977.

Mitchell, T.L. "Philistia." In *Archaeology and Old Testament Study*, ed. D. W. Thomas, 405-28. Oxford: Clarendon, 1967.

Moore, G.F. *A Critical and Exegetical Commentary on Judges*. New York: Charles Scribner's Sons, 1901.

Nel, Philip. "The Riddle of Samson (Judg 14,14,18)." *Bib* 66(1985) 534-45.

Niditch, Susan. *Judges: A Commentary*. Louisville: Westminster John Knox, 2008

———. "Samson as Culture Hero, Trickster, and Bandit: The Empowerment of the Weak." *CBQ* 52(1990) 608-24.

Noth, Martin. *The Deuteronomistic History*. JSOTSup 15. Sheffield: JSOT, 1981.

O'Connell, Robert H. *The Rhetoric of the Book of Judges*. VTSup 63. Leiden: Brill, 1966.

Olson, D.T. "Judges." In *NIB* 2:721-888. Nashville: Abingdon, 1988.

Oppenheim, A. L. *Ancient Mesopotamia*. Chicago: University of Chicago Press, 1964.

Ovid, *Metamorphoses*. Translated by Frank Justus Miller. Cambridge Massachusetts: Harvard University Press, 1916.

Palmer, A. Smythe. *The Samson-Saga*. London: Sir Isaac Pitman& Sons, 1913.

Paul, Shalom. *Amos*. Minneapolis: Fortress, 1991.

Pausanias. *Description of Greece*. Translated by W.H. Jones, Litt.D. Cambridge, Massachusetts: Harvard University Press, 1935.

———. "Plowing with a Heifer in Judges 14:18: Tracing a Sexual Euphemism." In *Sacred History, Sacred Literature: Essays on Ancient Israel, the Bible, and Religion in Honor of R.E. Friedman on his Sixtieth Birthday*, edited by Shawna Dolansky, 163-67. Winona Lake, Indiana: Eisenbrauns, 2008.

Pfeiffer, Robert H. Translator. "Akkadian Proverbs and Counsels." In *ANET*, 425-27.

Porter, J.R. "Samson's Riddle: Judges XIV.14, 18." *JThS* 13(1962) 106-9.

Von Rad, Gerhard. *Old Testament Theology*. Translated by D. M. Stalker. New York: Harper & Brothers, 1962.

Bibliography

Reinhartz, A. "Samson's Mother: An Unnamed Protagonist." *JSTOR* 55(1992) 25-37.
Robertson Smith, W. *Lectures on the Religion of the Semites*. London: Adam and Charles Black, 1901.
Römer, Thomas. *The So-Called Deuteronomistic History*. New York: T&T Clark, 2007.
Samueli, Haim. "Samson's Riddle." In *Kornegrin Book*, 57-63 Tell Aviv: Niv, 1964. (Hebrew)
Sasson, Jack M. "Who Cut Samson Hair? (And Other Trifling Issues Raised by Judges 16)." *Proof* 8(1988) 333-46.
———. "A Genealogical >>Convention<< in Biblical Chronography?" *ZAW* 90(1978) 171-85.
Scheiber, A. "Samson Uprooting a Tree." *JQR* 50(1959-1960) 176-80.
———."Further Parallels to the Figure of Samson the Tree-Uprooter." *JQR* 52(1961-1962) 35-40.
Schunck, K.D. "סרן srn." In *TDOT* 10:350-53.
Segert, Stanislav. "Paronomasia in the Samson Narrative Judges XIII- XVI." *VT* 34(1984) 454-61.
Van Seters, J. *Abraham in History and Tradition*. New Haven, CT: Yale University Press, 1975
Simon, U "Samson and the Heroic." In *Ways of Reading the Bible,* edited by M. Wadsworth, 154-67. London: Sussex, 1981.
Simpson, Cuthbert Aikman. *Composition of the Book of Judges*. Oxford: Basil Blackwell, 1958.
Skinner, John. *A Critical and Exegetical Commentary on Genesis*. New York: Charles Scribner's sons, 1910.
Soggin, Alberto. J. *Judges*. Translated by John Bowden. Philadelphia: Westminster, 1981.
Speiser, E.A. *Genesis*. AB 1. Garden City New York: Doubleday, 1964.
Stager, Lawrence E. "Forging an Identity: The Emergence of Ancient Israel." In *The Oxford History of the Biblical World,* edited by Michael D. Coogan, 123-75. New York: Oxford University Press, 1998.
Theocritus. *Idyll*. Edited with Translation and Commentary by A.S.F. Gow. Cambridge: Cambridge University Press, 1950.
Van der Toorn. "Theology, Priests, and Worship in Canaan and Ancient Israel." In *Civilization of the Ancient Near East*, edited by Jack. M. Sasson, 3:2043-58. New York: Charles Scribner's Sons, 1995.
Tsevat, Matitiahu. "Was Samuel a Nazirite?" In *Sha'arei Talmon*, edited by Michael Fishbane and Emanuel Tov with the assistance of Weston W. Fields, 199-204. Winona Lake, Indiana: Eisenbrauns, 1992.
Tur-Sinai, N.H. "Riddle in the Bible." In *Halson vahSefer*, 58-93. Jerusalem: Bialik, 1959. (Hebrew).
Yadin, Azzan. "Samson's Ḥîdâ." *VT* 52(2002) 407-26
Yadin, Y. "And Dan, why did he remain in ships." *AJBA* 1(1968) 9-23.
———. "Goliath's Javelin and מנור אורגים." *PEQ* 87(1955) 58-69.
Yahuda, S. "The Meaning of the Name Esther." *JRAS* 8(1946) 174-78.
Vander Kam, James C. *Enoch and the Growth of the Apocalyptic Tradition*. Washington DC: The Catholic Biblical Association of America, 1984.
de Vaux, Roland. *Ancient Israel* its *Life and Institutions*. Translated by John Mchugh. London: Darton, Longman& Todd, 1961.
———. *The Early History of Israel*. Trans. David Smith. Philadelphia: Westminster, 1978.
Webb, Barry G. *The Book of Judges*. Grand Rapids Michigan: William B. Eerdmans, 2012.

Bibliography

Wellhausen, J. *Reste arabischen Heidentums: gesammelt und erläutert. Dritte unveränderte Auflage.* Berlin: Walter de Gruyter & Co., 1961.

Virgil, *Georgics.* Translated by H. Rushton Fairclough. Cambridge, Massachusetts: Harvard University Press, 1932.

Wiseman, D. "Abraham Reassessed." In *Essays on the Patriarchal Narratives*, ed. A. R. Millard and D.J. Wiseman, 141-60. Winona Lake, IN: Eisenbrauns, 1983.

Wyatt, N. "Astarte." In *DDD*, 109-14.

Zakovitch Y. *The Life of Samson.* Jerusalem: Magnes, 1982.(Hebrew).

Scripture Index

HEBREW BIBLE

Genesis

Reference	Page
2:19	11
3:8	9
5:24	84
6:1–4	16
7:17	3
10:9	85
10:14	98
15:2	117
15:8	117
17:9–14	54
18:3	5
18:8	11
18:32	117
21:20	13
25:21	4
25:22	5
25: 24–26	13
26:1	107
26:26	57
29:20–23	61
29:22	57
29:27	56
30:22	5
32:22–32	11
32:30	11
33: 31	12
34:4	53
38:13	55
38:17	55
38:24	55
41	114
49:9	87
49:16–18	xvii
49:18	112
49:26	30
50:8	120
50:13	120

Exodus

Reference	Page
2:11	13
3:6	12
3:13	11
3:14	74
12:43–9	54
24:18	3
29:40	32
34:28	3

Leviticus

Reference	Page
5:2	22
5:14–16	23
6:9	22
9:6–7	22
10:1	12
10:9	24
11:8	28
17:15	28
20:14	58
21:9	58

Scripture Index

Numbers

6: 1–21	xxi
6:2	56
6:3	5
6:3–8	20
6:5	20
6:6–7	22
6:9, 18	21
11:10–15	119
12:8	73
13:3	16
14:33–4	3
15:5	32
20:8	45
21	110
21:17	114
21:27	72
23:24	87
24:24	98
26:42	3
28:14	32
32:13	3

Deuteronomy

2:6	5
2:23	98
3:3	114
3:24	117
4:19	14
9:18	2
9:26	117
10:10	3
7:1–5	54
7:25	110
14:21	28
14:26	32
16:19	120
17:2	2
17:3	14
21:1–9	9
23:10–14	30
24:3	61
29:5	5
31: 29	2
32:42	30
33:16	30
33:22	87

Joshua

2:1	47
2:2	47
2:5	47
2:16, 22, 23	47
2:24	114
3:5	30
6:22	47
8:20	12
19:43	53

Judges

1:19	104
1:34	99
2:6–16	xvi
3:9	1
3:11	2
3:31	xvi, 100
4:4	xvi
4:21	xxii
5:2	30
5:31	2
6:11–24	2, 37
6:15	xvii
6:22	12
6:39	117
7:13	74
7:16–19	92
8:28	2
8:31	38
9:8–15	65
11:1, 30–40	121
12:1	58
13:1	xvi, 2
13:2–24	xxi, 36, 37
13:4, 7, 14	24
13:5	xvi, 33
13:7	28, 33
13:9	9
13:15	11
13:18	11
13:20	92
13:24	13
13:25	3, 96
14:1	52
14:1–15.8	xxi, 52
14:2	53

Scripture Index

14:4	69	10:5	101
14:5	55	11:6–7	50
14:6, 19	50	12: 3	120
14:9	25	13:3, 11	101
14:10, 12, 17	20	13:5	104
14:11–12	100	14:14	50
14:14	74	14:15	104
14:15	55	14:27	94
14:16–18	51	16:7	119
15:1	55, 59	16:14	50
15:4–5	90	16:20	10
15:14	96	17:36	50
5:17	xv	18:7	114
15:18	117	18:19	61
15:20	123	18:27	101
16:1	47	18:30	101
16:2	47	19:8	101
16:3	47	21:5–6	30
16:5	116	21:11	103
16:6	65	21:12	114
16:7	33	22:11	103
16:19	68	23:1–5	101
16:23, 25	20	24:1	101
16:24	115	27:2	103
16:30	51	27:5	103
16:31	123	29:1, 30–31	101
17:6	xvi, 54	29:2	104
17:10	127	29:4–10	103
18:1	127	29:5	114
18:27	100	30:12	5
19:1	127	31:4	51
20:40	12	31:7	101
21:9	xv	31:8–13	109
21:25	xvi, 54, 127		

1 Samuel

1:1	3
1:11	xxi, 29
1:17	5
2:21	120
3:19	13
4: 1–7	101
4:18	3
5:1–7	108
5:2–4	108
6:4	110
7:9–14	32
9:15	50

2 Samuel

1:10	30
1:13	7
2:8–9	101
5:17–24	101
5:21	110
5:25	101
6:21	116
8:1	101
8:18	101
11:11	30
13:28	115
14:6	9
14:25–26	22

Scripture Index

2Samuel *(cont.)*

14:26	22
15:18–22	101
20:7, 23	101
21:18–22	101
22:14	84
23:9–17	101
23:11–12	88
23:13–14	101
23:20–21	86

1Kings

1:38, 44	102
2:11	3
2:39–40	102
10:1	71, 72
13:24–28	85
19:4	119
20:36	85

2Kings

1:2, 3, 6, 16	108
5:5, 22	74
11:12	30
17:16	95
21:5	95
23:11	95

Isaiah

3:23	74
7:14	5
28:7	24
48:21	45
56:11	81

Jeremiah

1	8
2:30	75
7:12, 14	101
19:13	
20:17	119
25:30	86
35:65	31
47:4	98

Ezekiel

3:3	75
8:16	95
17:1	72
17:2	71
25: 16	98
43:3	73
44:20	24
44:21	24

Hosea

4:19	84
12:11	73

Joel

4:16	86

Amos

1:2	86
2:11–12	31
3:4–8	86
9:7	98

Jonah

4:8	67

Zephaniah

2:5	98

Psalms

19:11	75
49:5	72
68:5	84
74:16	95
78:2	72
78:15–16	45
83:10–12	xvii
99:6	27
105:41	45

Proverbs

1:5–6	72
24:13	75

Scripture Index

30:25	75	**Nehemiah**	
31:24	74	9:15	45
Job		**1 Chronicle**	
9:7	59	4:3	4
31:26–27	95	9:29	32
		10:10	108
Ecclesiastes		11:12–19	101
6:4	81	11:22	86
19:3	81	14:8–17	101
		14:12	110
		18:11	101
Esther		18:17	102
1:10–11	115		
7:10	xxii	**2 Chronicle**	
		26	103
Daniel			
8:23	72		

APOCRYPHA

I Esdars
3: 13–41   72

NEW TESTAMENT

Matthew
10:25   109
12:24   109

Mark
3:22   109

Luke
11:15   109

Hebrew
11:32   xvii

www.ingramcontent.com/pod-product-compliance
Lightning Source LLC
Chambersburg PA
CBHW071506150426
43191CB00009B/1436